SOPHOCLES TO FUGARD

BRIAN STONE AND PAT SCORER

Sophocles to Fugard

BRITISH BROADCASTING CORPORATION

Published by the
British Broadcasting Corporation,
35 Marylebone High Street, London W1M 4AA

ISBN 0 563 17267 3

First published 1977

© Brian Stone and Pat Scorer 1977

Printed in England by Butler & Tanner Ltd, Frome and London

We gratefully acknowledge the co-operation of the Open University, which gave permission for the television programmes to be used as the basis of this book. The sixteen programmes were made for the course team for *A307: Drama*, of which Brian Stone is Chairman.

We thank the BBC for placing its materials and resources at our disposal, and Peter Dunkley, BBC Editor, Arts Programmes, Open University, for encouraging and promoting our work with energy and sympathy. We acknowledge with thanks the work of David Amey, who directed the photography for the illustrations for all the programmes except the last. The photographs of *Sizwe Bansi is Dead* are by John Haynes.

We should like particularly to thank the four television directors of the plays, Richard Callanan, John Selwyn Gilbert, Paul Kafno and Nick Levinson, for their detailed collaboration: this book is in some measure a testimonial to their work.

Pat Scorer
Brian Stone

CONTENTS

Introduction

This book introduces to the interested viewing public sixteen fifty-minute television drama programmes produced in the BBC's Studio A at Alexandra Palace for the Open University's course *A307: Drama*. The course is principally concerned with modern drama, to which eleven of the sixteen programmes are devoted. Two, the sixth and seventh programmes, illustrate its beginnings: Büchner's *Woyzeck* (1837), which anticipated, fifty years before Ibsen, characteristically modern dramatic preoccupations and tone, and Jarry's *Ubu Roi* (1896), which with its ruthless iconoclasm, absurdities and obscenities, prompted a studio technician working on the production to remark: 'I didn't know they had *Monty Python* in the 1890s!' Six further programmes present plays by Ibsen, Chekhov, Strindberg, Pirandello and Brecht, the acknowledged masters of modern European drama. And the last three show plays written in the last quarter of a century, by Beckett, Genet and Fugard; they are strictly plays of our times, reflecting contemporary concerns and attitudes through contemporary sensibilities.

The modern drama, which we think of as beginning in the late nineteenth century, is approached in this series through a historical perspective, because it can be best understood and enjoyed if we know something of the drama that preceded it. So the first five programmes are of plays from earlier periods. The ghosts of Sophocles (and Aeschylus and Euripides too, for that matter), from two thousand four hundred years ago, and Shakespeare, from four hundred years ago, tower over the shoulder of any dramatist in the Western world who sits down to write a serious play. Greek tragedies are often revived, reinterpreted and even used as material for new plays, and Shakespeare still dominates the European dramatic scene as well as being, in Britain at any rate, the surest box-office draw.

Sophocles's *Oedipus the King* selected itself not only because it is the best-known Greek tragedy, but because the Open University possessed a fine new translation by the Dean of the Arts Faculty, John Ferguson. We chose *Macbeth* not merely because it is the shortest of Shakespeare's tragedies, or because its two main characters so dwarf all the others that it was worth presenting in a condensed version. It is quintessential tragedy. The two deeply imagined characters of Macbeth and Lady Macbeth, expressing themselves in matchless dramatic poetry, move abhorred to their deaths, locked in a moralistic, yet mysteriously mocking, Fate. They scatter ever more terror as their disillusionment and despair increase, and their destiny develops in a rhythmic sweep of intense thought, feeling and, above all, action, which has the concentration and climax of performed ritual; ritual, in which drama originated among the Greeks.

The third programme presents two short medieval religious plays, a genre which has been somewhat neglected by historians of the drama. But it was, after all, the main kind of drama publicly performed in Europe for the four hundred years up to 1550, and the Christian consciousness it expresses remains with us. More important still, its theatrical practices and social function continue to influence today's progressive and avant-garde theatre: it was a community drama, and its free but precise use of varied performing spaces, its bold conventions harmonising the realistic, the abstract and the supernatural, its technical ingenuity and its classlessness, commend it to contemporary drama groups trying to escape the rigid, classbound proscenium theatre of urban Western Europe.

Comedy and its grotesque image, farce, even as we know them, are also rooted in theatrical and literary practices which have developed over two and a half thousand years, though in rather different ways from tragedy. The latter seems an absolute: there is no need to render *Oedipus* and *Macbeth* into twentieth-century idiom, because they stand for all time in their universals. But comedy, even the romantic comedy of Shakespeare, which is not represented in this series, seems to depend more heavily on topicality; to contain specific social criticism of its own age, and to laugh at or with contemporary types of character. So, although the character types, the sorts of plot and details of intrigue, and the social relevance are constants, they have new variants in every age. Accordingly, in our fourth and fifth programmes we present two kinds of comedy, each of which represents a late and, from our point of view, ideal stage of development in a long tradition reaching back to Greece and Rome. The first tradition is the non-literary one of farce; fast-moving plays in which stock characters – young lovers, fussy old men of various kinds, bragging soldiers, intriguing servants – get involved in all sorts of intrigues about love and money, with the kinds of slapstick 'business' that we now associate with circus, music-hall and, to some extent, French bedroom farce. In the eighteenth century Goldoni took that kind of play, which had up to his time been largely improvised, and converted it into a formal play: *The Venetian Twins* was the result. But whether literary or not, the play represents a tradition of comedy and of comic acting which will never die, one that light-heartedly explores the absurdities and incongruities that encrust our frame of serious life.

The second comic tradition was the literary one, which depended much more on verbal wit and deeper social analysis, but also drew on stock types and complicated intrigue. Its best practitioners before the modern period began were probably Molière in France and Ben Jonson in England. In this series Congreve is represented because he is the most polished English writer in the comedy of manners mode, and because his tone and subject-matter seem nearer to our own than those of Ben Jonson. Also, he was preferred to Molière, who is much the greater dramatist, because in a kind of comedy which is dependant on verbal wit we thought it essential to broadcast a play in its original language. Congreve, whose *The Way of the World* was staged in 1700, was as it happens deeply influenced by Molière. To our great regret, we were unable to include a play by Shaw, whose wit, theatrical craft and purposeful zeal have in our own century turned the comedy of manners into a new and significant kind of drama.

We do not propose to explain or justify the inclusion of plays by Ibsen, Chekhov, Strindberg, Pirandello, Brecht and Beckett, the important dramatists whose work is featured in seven programmes (nos. 8–14); but the choice of Genet and Fugard for the last two programmes may interest people who are aware of the many good plays and different kinds of play that might have been chosen. We thought it best to present unusual plays which enlarge the understanding rather than anything at all orthodox. Genet and Fugard are of course completely different in outlook. Genet is anarchic and Fugard pleads constructively for humane values; but each in his own way approaches the expression of his vision theatrically. Genet stretches to the utmost the capacity of the theatre to convey illusion: mirrors, Chinese-box effects of role-playing – role within role – masks, stilted figures, contrived and complicated stage settings. Genet's dialogue is highly wrought and often richly poetic, an effect partly lost in translation. Fugard concentrates on the actors in *Sizwe Bansi is Dead*: the stage is stripped of all ornament or suggestion, and the actors manage just their essential props; the written dialogue exists only as a basis upon which the actors erect each performance, which depends entirely on a single acting relationship. It is what Grotowski might well accept as ideal 'Poor Theatre.'

That goes some way, we hope, towards explaining our choices, but there were other considerations, some of them practical, which are worth declaring. To begin with, the television programmes are for a University course which contains forty plays,★ and so it was essential to have sixteen programmes which fairly represented the scope of the course as a whole. Then, since there are so many different kinds of play, we thought it important for every play to be of a different kind; we should not include two Shakespearian tragedies or two realistic Ibsen plays, for example. Next, there was the limit of fifty minutes per programme, which meant that unless a play could be shortened or represented reasonably by a coherent fifty-minute extract, it would not be included. Lastly, there were two non-academic and decidedly worldly considerations which affected our choices: costs and copyright. The first meant that we could not consider a play with a huge cast, or one which absolutely necessitated ponderous design commitments, and the second

★The full list of plays, in order of study, is: Pinter: *Silence*; Sophocles: *Oedipus the King, Oedipus at Colonus;* Euripides: *The Bacchae;* Shakespeare: *Macbeth;* Medieval Mystery Plays: The Wakefield *Second Shepherds' Pageant*, the Chester *Noah*, the York *Crucifixion*, the Brome *Abraham and Isaac; The Castle of Perseverance*; Goldoni: *The Venetian Twins*; Shakespeare: *Twelfth Night*; Molière: *Tartuffe*; Congreve: *The Way of the World*; Jarry: *Ubu Roi*; Büchner: *Woyzeck*; Ibsen: *Peer Gynt, Rosmersholm*; Euripides: *Alcestis*; Shakespeare: *The Winter's Tale*; Ibsen: *The Wild Duck*; Chekhov: *Three Sisters, The Cherry Orchard*; Strindberg: *Miss Julie, The Ghost Sonata*; Pirandello: *Six Characters in Search of an Author*; Shaw: *Major Barbara, Saint Joan*; Brecht: *Galileo, Mother Courage and her Children, The Exception and the Rule*; Otway: *Venice Preserved*, Arden: *Serjeant Musgrave's Dance*; Beckett: *Waiting for Godot:* Weiss: *The Marat-Sade*; Genet: *The Balcony*; Bond: *Lear*; Fugard: *Sizwe Bansi is Dead*.

meant that certain modern plays could not be included simply because they were not made available to us.

Although the plays chosen were written for several different kinds of theatre – and in the case of *Peer Gynt*, for no theatre at all – every production except that of *Sizwe Bansi is Dead*, which was an existing BBC programme, was mounted in Studio A at Alexandra Palace. This is a small studio, the first ever to be used in British television, and the budget was moderate. Accordingly, a studio style was built up through the series, and functional, economic sets were used. Nevertheless, in some of the programmes extraordinary effects of illusion and space are achieved, and there is no sense of standardisation – that is to say in style of acting, design and directing – because of the ample variety in presentation method. The concentration on acting and absence of clutter make for dramatic force and clarity, and curiously enough the limit of programme length to fifty minutes was felt less as a drawback than as a means of wonderfully concentrating the minds of the production team.

Television, the medium which takes these plays to viewers and is now the chief drama medium in the world, is electronic artefact. What you see on the screen and what you hear are the products of highly sophisticated engineering at the production end and a properly adjusted receiver of good quality at your end. Television drama suffers extraordinarily if the set is a bad one or is not tuned properly – you cannot see the detail of the faces, the colours are wrong, there are ghost lines round outlines, or blurs, or sudden contrast changes.

Studio drama production is a highly technical art form in its own right. The director commands a team of about sixty people, and every decision he makes is based on technical as well as artistic considerations. His rehearsal from the outset is conceived in terms of camera shots, in addition to all the other criteria of drama production – interpretation, visual and aural pattern and effect, grouping, rhythm, pace and so on. For any given moment in a play the director has decided which camera (of three or four, depending on the layout of the studio set and the requirements of the action) has its shots recorded, and what sort of shot it is (for example, close-up, medium close-up, full-length, or long shot), as well as from what angle it is taken (front-face, profile, high-angle, or low-angle), and whether it shows the speaker or the listener, or both, or a group of people. He makes his camera-cutting – that is, the changing of shot from one camera to another – an aesthetic instrument which achieves a distinctive effect for the play he is directing: in *Oedipus the King*, a majestic tragedy, there are fewer than two hundred shot changes in the fifty minutes, but in *The Venetian Twins*, a fast-moving farce, there are more than four hundred.

A play shot in a studio is not now presented 'live'. After a fortnight or so of rehearsal elsewhere, it is shot sequence by sequence in the most convenient order. As far as possible, the original order of the play is followed in the shooting, so that the character interpretation may develop naturally. A sequence may be shot several times before all technical and artistic details are just right and the director is satisfied. Sometimes actors will ask for a sequence to be shot again because they think they can do it better: sometimes the director will refrain from shooting again a sequence that he thinks imperfect because he judges that the actors have given all they could. When the three days of hard studio rehearsal and shooting are over, the director still has to edit the whole of the material to refine the effects he is seeking and to get the timing exactly right. Probably he also has to add sound effects, music if any, and opening titles and closing credits, together with the visual and sound effects these require.

The director of such a complex operation controls matters by well-established routines, and like the leader of any big team or group, he sets the tone and determines the morale for the whole production group, as well as providing the framework within which distinguished professionals of diverse accomplishment may achieve their artistic goals. It is a myth that drama people are erratic in behaviour. The politeness in the control gallery, which has direct communication with every technician working on the programme, was always absolute. No request was made without 'please' or some equivalent; no job was done without the doer being thanked. And the best-known actors were usually the most technically aware and the least temperamental. Many famous and experienced actors and actresses played parts in this series, and enjoyed working at Alexandra Palace, where they found an unusual dedication to the job in hand, a friendly spirit and remarkable co-operation.

This drama series made demands on all staff – production, design, costume, make-up, camera, sound and special effects among them – beyond any other series of programmes made for the Open University, and thus well beyond what the staffing complement was intended to achieve. For example, the designer of *Peer Gynt*, the last programme to be made, lost a stone in weight over the four weeks of active preparation – and he was quite lean to begin with.

If this little book draws attention to the fine work done, and to the great plays worked on, it will have been worth the writing.

Oedipus the King by Sophocles
Translated by John Ferguson
The second half of the play from line 769 to the end is performed.

Oedipus	Patrick Stewart
Jocasta	Rosalie Crutchley
First Chorus	Derek Godfrey
Second Chorus	Joe Melia
Corinthian Shepherd	Ronald Radd
Theban Shepherd	John Citroen
Palace Attendant	Roy Marsden
Creon	John Forbes-Robertson
Music	Judith Bingham
Choreographer	Jonathan Taylor
Designer	Dacre Punt
Director	Richard Callanan

Illustration: *Oedipus (Patrick Stewart) with his two daughters after the blinding.*

Sophocles
Oedipus the King
(c. 429–426 BC)

Greek tragedy was performed as part of the spring rituals in honour of Dionysus, the god of wine, vegetation and fertility, in huge theatres where actors, chorus and audience were united by the ceremonial spirit of the occasion under the open sky and in a natural setting. The Theatre of Dionysus at Athens, where *Oedipus* and all the other Greek tragedies of which we have any real knowledge were first performed, was on the hillside below the Acropolis, and could hold an audience of about 14,000, all of whom would be men. They would be ranged in a tiered semicircle round the northern half of the *orchestra*, or dancing-place, a circular area sixty feet across with an altar in the centre and a long facade, or stage-building as it is called, to the south.

The form of the play, and the style of its presentation, derived from the choruses sung and danced in the god's worship. The commonest form was of five sections, each with a choral ode and an acted episode, with entry and final exit choruses. The whole was performed continuously, but nevertheless gave a standard form of five acts to most of the plays written in Renaissance Europe, and many in succeeding times. As for the style, we must envisage a numerous chorus masked and costumed alike, singing and intoning, and also ritually moving and dancing, in the *orchestra*, while in front of the stage-building the characters, played by masked actors wearing padded costumes, who appeared almost statuesque, moved and spoke in tragic conflict. The choruses were often citizens, as in *Oedipus the King*, but might be groups of strange beings, such as Furies or Bacchantes. They were always of people involved in the action, and sometimes they were so important that they provide the titles of plays, as in *The Bacchae* of Euripides.

The ritual performance – a solemn one in a festival which contained ecstatic and orgiastic elements – was enhanced by spectacular effects: thunder machines, billowing smoke, burning torches, and crane-like devices for hoisting divine or magically endowed beings through the air on chariots. So we should think of the performance of a Greek tragedy as something like a service combining the qualities of grand opera, ballet, majestic verse drama and high mass, conducted in a great open-air stadium holding four times as many people as the London Coliseum.

A drama like this, so strange and powerful, poses problems for a modern director in the theatre or television studio, because he must find convincing equivalents for elements foreign to the tradition and the milieu within which he works. And the beholder, for his part, whether in theatre or sitting-room, must make the kind of imaginative leap that will help him to understand and empathise with a drama which, however bizarre, is, like all great art, rooted in profound human experience.

The great mythological figure of Oedipus is the subject of the best-known ancient Greek tragedy. Briefly, here is the story, which concerns man's struggle with the inscrutable will of the gods – or Fate, if you like – and with the incest taboo:

The parents of Oedipus, King Laius and Queen Jocasta of Thebes, warned by the oracle of Apollo that their son will kill his father, arrange to have him killed while still a baby. But the shepherd who is to expose him, in pity gives him away, and he is reared by King Polybus of Corinth. When Oedipus grows up, hearing the prophecy that he will kill his father and marry his mother, he flees the court and his imagined parents in horror. Arriving near Thebes, he kills a man at a cross-roads in a stupid quarrel over the right of way: it is his real father. He then finds Thebes terrorised by the Sphinx, solves her riddle and so defeats her, and marries the mourning queen, by whom he has four children. The play begins with Thebes in the grip of a plague, and with an instruction from Apollo that the plague will cease only when Thebes rids itself of the source of pollution. Oedipus resolves to root out the pollution. Arrogantly confident of his virtue and powers as ruler, and disregarding both direct warnings and ominous signs that the search for the truth will harm him, he conducts a series of interrogations which at last bring out the facts: he killed his father, he married and had children by his mother, and so he is accursed to gods and human kind. Jocasta hangs herself; Oedipus puts out his own eyes and goes into exile in horror and self-loathing.

A barbaric, violent and pitiless affair. Yet this is the play by Sophocles (*c.* 496–406 BC) that Aristotle used as main basis for his theory of tragedy, which has so much influenced all serious Western drama since the fourth century BC. It is also the play which, through its mythical subject-matter and its dramatic treatment, is so important in the thinking of Freud, the Viennese founder of modern psychology. Probably many of us first hear the name of Oedipus in the phrase 'the Oedipus complex'. Perhaps most important of all, *Oedipus the King* stands with *King Lear* and the *Book of Job* as a masterwork on human suffering and divine providence. Job was a just man, who suffered eloquently and heroically as God tested his faith. Lear, though not blameless, suffered titanically but died with his capacity for love and harmony restored. Oedipus, though to us he seems blameless for the pollution of incest, was guilty of *hubris*, that is, of arrogant pride in face of the gods (because he thought that, by forth-right action, he could prevent the fulfilment of the prophecy): hence his greater sense of guilt when he discovers the truth. Job had all restored to him: in this play Oedipus retires comfortless, and it was twenty years before Sophocles, in writing Oedipus at Colonus (406 BC) at the very end of his life, celebrated his hero's comparative innocence, his atonement through suffering, and his elevation to something like a Greek equivalent of sainthood.

To understand and enjoy *Oedipus the King*, we must first come to terms with the kind of life and world-view expressed in the play. Classical civilisation, for all its marvellous achievements, was closer in modes of feeling, thought and social organisation to its primitive roots than our industrial and largely godless society. Private and public life were governed by traditional sanctities and certainties. Under the rule of the gods, which people somehow expected to be just but often found arbitrary, there were common assumptions about the bonds and duties of kinship – relations between husband and wife, parent and child, brother and sister; and about the social order – the relation between ruler and realm, man and master, citizen and citizen, and man and the gods. In the drama individual passions, generally more intense than those met in modern plays, fought for expression within this high-principled but inflexible scheme of things.

In the television programme, the second half of *Oedipus Tyrannus* (the King) is performed. The studio set, by offering just an altar and a palace door in a wall against a light blue cyclorama, aims at the right sort of open-air, perhaps hill-top, atmosphere. The transparent half-masks are designed deliberately to restrict facial expression and so help to produce a studio equivalent of stylised Greek acting. With this goes a formal way of speaking which emphasises the meaning, but underplays the violence and emotional turbulence of the dialogue. This distancing effect, with its cumulative impact, paradoxically fosters our power to identify with the feelings of the characters. In such a convention, Oedipus's silent mimed scream when the truth comes out does the work of a realistic howl, and the controlled dignity of the Palace Attendant's subsequent narration of Jocasta's suicide and Oedipus's self-blinding – a beautiful figure recounting horrors – helps us to focus on what is almost unbearable. Patrick Stewart's Oedipus, at first masterful and articulate, then silently overwhelmed by the revelation of his guilt of flesh and spirit, is nicely balanced at the climax by the pained awareness of Roy Marsden as the Palace Attendant. His controlled bearing reminds one of the manner in which Jocasta, played by Rosalie Crutchley, retired with dignity into the palace to end her own life once she had recognised, well before all other members of the court, the approach of terrible and unbearable truth. Only the two shepherds, counterpointing the high tragedy with their down-to-earth speech and sympathies, suggest naturalism.

As is common in modern productions of Greek tragedy, the members of the Chorus speak singly and not in unison; but in other respects their group function is emphasised. They are in black and white, in contrast to the deep reds and purples of the other characters. Their delivery is that of the main characters, not the shepherds. They move in a rhythmic and stylised dance mode, which gradually becomes more agitated and

The Theban Shepherd (John Citroen) confronting the Chorus, led by Derek Godfrey.

expressive as the events of the play unfold. The climax is the entry of Oedipus blinded, in a dark red mask which symbolises the blood and pollution. It is prepared for by Jocasta's withdrawal into the palace after she has failed to persuade Oedipus to stop his investigations. She goes with her face and body curiously crooked in her grief and self-disgust. This seeming physical distortion is taken up again in the face of the Theban shepherd who tells Oedipus the clinching truth; and its final effect – the physical ugliness expressing the spiritual distress and evil – is achieved when Oedipus staggers on in the agony of his self-mutilation.

The impact of the play depends on faithful representation of its central idea. Whatever we moderns think of the kind of Greek justice portrayed, Jocasta and Oedipus felt guilty; not simply betrayed by the gods. Aristotle wrote of tragedy that, by means of pity and fear, it brings about the purgation of such emotions. At the end of *Oedipus Tyrannus*, whatever other 'such emotions' exist, we certainly feel pity as Oedipus retires into the palace weighed down with pain, and with guilt and horror at his life of incest. As his two daughter-sisters go out, their thin frames and tiny bare shoulders viewed from the back seem to provide a fitting image of human frailty. Oedipus is the more to be pitied because, even with the arrogance that led him to crime and self-banishment in guilt and self-loathing, he showed himself capable of statesmanship and ennobling love.

Jocasta (Rosalie Crutchley) tries to persuade Oedipus to stop his investigations.

Macbeth by William Shakespeare
The programme retains the narrative and dramatic line of the play and
concentrates on the relationship between Macbeth and Lady Macbeth.

Macbeth	Corin Redgrave
Lady Macbeth	Ann Bell
Duncan	Richard Beale
Banquo	John Golightly
Macduff	Mark Penfold
Lennox	Anthony Gardner
Rosse	John Lawrence
Witches	Aimée Delamain
	Hope Jackman
	Susan Thomas
Malcolm	Michael Mundell
Donalbain	Stuart Doughty
The Porter	Eric Chitty
The Doctor	Arthur Hewlett
The Gentlewoman	Hope Jackman
Designer	George Wisner
Director	Paul Kafno

Illustration: *The Witches' incantation over the royal death's-head.*

Macbeth (1606)

To most educated people, Shakespearian tragedy is as familiar as Greek tragedy is strange. Yet the kind of Elizabethan play that we studied at school, and saw or acted in if we were lucky, is just as extraordinary and complicated a work of art as *Oedipus the King*. All the conventions of Greek tragedy harmoniously fitted the public ritual occasion by the altar. The plays of William Shakespeare (1564–1616) were performed in a playhouse as a commercial venture, and among their conventions was this apparent inconsistency: the acting is naturalistic, that is to say, characters behave more or less as in real life, but the language they speak is the most subtle and forceful poetry. Shakespeare approved of natural delivery and naturalistic acting, as we know from Hamlet's speech to the Players visiting the Danish court:

> Suit the action to the word, the word to the action;
> with this special observance, that you o'erstep not
> the modesty of nature. (III. ii. 17–19)

Shakespeare's theatre took little account of place. In the ritual-istic drama of Sophocles the altar, orchestra and building-front at the back of the stage which were permanent, were also real within the play. But in the Elizabethan theatre the acting area, of spacious stage or fore-stage, upper stage and inner stage, gave just space and different levels, suggesting to the audience nothing but 'Here you see a play!' Only the doors by which the actors entered were 'real', because they were practical.

Locations were simply mentioned or described if the action made it necessary, and essential properties, like thrones, tables and beds were brought on, or revealed on the inner stage. This free space convention went with an equally free time convention: whereas the events of a Greek tragedy happened in not much more imagined time than real performing time, the action of a Shakespearian play might take months or even years of imagined time. All this we accept happily. That we do so is the best recommendation we can have to learn and accept other, and different, dramatic conventions.

Macbeth is the tragedy of a man who kills his king hoping to enjoy power and rule, but finds the consequence is more crime, universal detestation, loneliness and the loss of his wife, and death. Although in these islands it is hundreds of years since a king (or prime minister for that matter) was murdered and succeeded by his murderer, such things still happen in the world at large, and were common in Renaissance Europe. Shakespeare expresses in *Macbeth* the deep contradiction in the Renaissance world-view. On the one hand, centuries of Christianity had established the ideal vision, made up of high morality and social justice under the rule of a beneficent God who cared for every human being. This was much less barbaric than the one towards which people could strive under the Greek system, which offered no certain way of pleasing the gods. On the other hand, for whatever historic reasons, an aristocratic ideal of ambitious aspiration permeated the thought and action of Renaissance times. Naturally, if this motive was governed by really Christian morality, things might not turn out too badly; but if not, then excessive aspiration, the desire to reach the top at all costs, undermined private and public morality. In *Macbeth* Shakespeare dramatises the process, concentrating on the effect that murder and subsequent guilt have on a man of vivid imagination deeply imbued with humane ideals.

There are many problems in adapting Shakespeare for television. But the most prized quality of the Elizabethan theatre, close contact between actor and audience, which is frustrated by the existence of the proscenium arch in most of today's theatres, is fostered and even enhanced by the prime means by which television drama communicates. This is the audial and visual close-up which, sensitively directed (the television director *selects* every shot), achieves a focus on the performance, its meaning and mood, more accurate and forceful than the stage can—though of course there is no theatre ambience. You can hear all the words perfectly, whether they are whispered or bellowed; the voice thus has greater range and subtlety than in the theatre, where all depends on the actor's power to project. And you can see in magnified detail the working of face and gesture in soliloquy and dialogue, and the intimate juxtaposition and interplay of two or more characters in the passionate exchanges in which Shakespeare's plays are so rich. His dramatic poetry, supple, comprehensive in range of subject, register and tone, and powerful in its expression of human realities, might almost have been written for television. The medium can reinforce symbolic elements such as, in *Macbeth*, crown, cross, sword, death's-head; it can achieve satisfactory supernatural effects, as in the witches' and ghost scenes; it can provide appropriately extravagant costumes and significant musical effects; and, even in the small studio at Alexandra Palace, it can suggest wide space and far-ranging action, which are characteristically Shakespearian.

The problem of representing the essence of *Macbeth* in fifty minutes was eased by the overwhelming importance of the two main characters. Macbeth and Lady Macbeth are presented as fully as possible, within

Macbeth (Corin Redgrave) and Lady Macbeth (Ann Bell)
after the murder of Duncan.

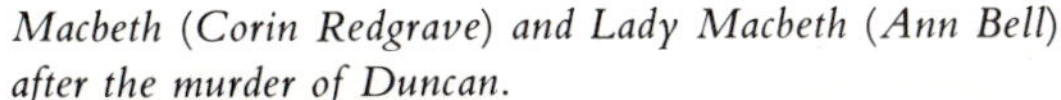

the frame of the main events of the play. Thus Act IV is omitted except for part of the last witches' scene and the report of the slaughter of Macduff's family, and minor characters and scenes of comment and general action are severely cut throughout; the programme ends with the death of Macbeth.

Macbeth is nothing unless the verse, with its range, resonance, haunting images and profound psychological insight, dominates the performance. Corin Redgrave's Macbeth is a man of imaginative introspection; his soliloquies and conversation with his wife avoid rhetoric and concentrate broodingly on meaning. Ann Bell complements his introspection with a dynamism which, without sapping the imperious force of her persuasions, is as softly delicate as her appearance. With this subdued interplay goes a deliberately slow camera-cutting which avoids the kinds of startling effect achieved in the witches' and other action scenes. The atmosphere of darkness which pervades the text is conveyed by the use of little or flickering light, and by allowing shadow on faces against dark, sometimes dark red, backgrounds, so that often the screen, with one or two sculptured faces in the foreground and rich darkness behind and around, looks Rembrandtesque.

The haunting force of the verse is supported by occasional presentation of terrible events, such as the moment when Banquo's ghost leaves the banqueting table and advances slowly on Macbeth. We experience that through Macbeth's eyes and ears – because nobody else is aware of the ghost's presence. The savage chopping to death of Banquo just before, and the pathetic exposure of Lady Macbeth's broken spirit in the sleep-walking scene, in which she seems to behave like a tormented child, give concrete as well as imaginative actuality to the general horror of the play.

But the particular horror of the crimes and death of Macbeth and his Lady forms the core of a play which is above all one of development: from the couple's conscious plunge into the first, irrevocable murder of their 'sainted king', Duncan, to their own hideously isolated deaths. Bound from the start by love, they extend their embrace to include an excited complicity in murder. But partners in life and crime though they may be, they are quite different as people. This Macbeth, who seems never to have been innocent or unambiguously virtuous, has to be lured sexually to commit the crime by his wife, whose passionate, ambitious and less scrupulous temperament dictates the easy pace of their early exchanges. Macbeth had been appalled at his own first thoughts of killing Duncan, while she had thrilled to the prospect of advancement and power.

The murder of Banquo (John Golightly).

With the murder accomplished, however, she slowly declines into distracted paralysis as she watches her husband diminish into nightmare-ridden defiance. Out of his defiance grows a trust in action. As Lady Macbeth disintegrates, to die mad at last, Macbeth moves ever faster from the idea of murder to actual killing of his enemies – Banquo, Macduff's family, and all the other unrecorded enemies for whom those stand. As human and supernatural forces mass against him, he is stripped of almost every quality but bravery and self-awareness, and becomes little more than an organism trying to survive. Through him, and to a lesser extent through Lady Macbeth, we are forced to savour the experience of being entirely caught up in a drama of evil and its consequences.

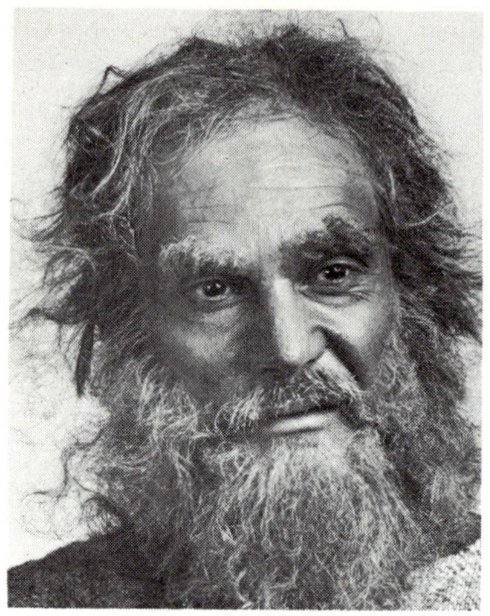 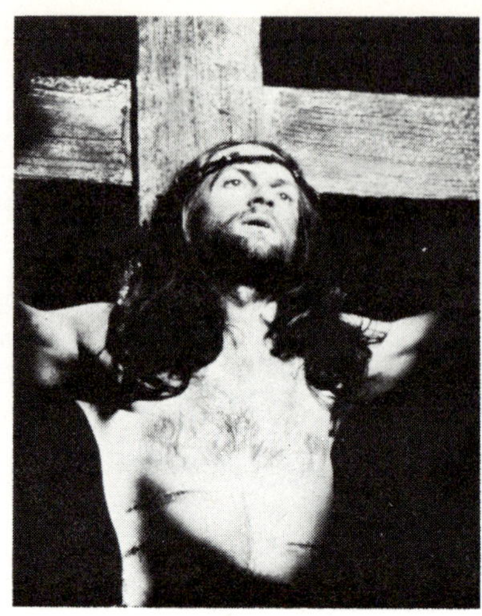

MEDIEVAL MYSTERY PLAYS
The Brome *Abraham and Isaac* and the York *Crucifixion*
Late fifteenth-century texts edited by Brian Stone
The plays are performed in full and spoken in a reconstruction of the
original dialect.

Abraham and Isaac
Abraham   Daniel Massey
Isaac   Gary Carp
God   Ken Parry
Angel   Ian Oliver

The Crucifixion
Christ   John Moreno
Sergeant   William Maxwell
Oswald   George Little
Thomas   Declan Mulholland
Nicholas   Ian Oliver

Designer   Steve Scott
Director   Nick Levinson

Illustrations: *Daniel Massey as Abraham. John Moreno as Christ.*

The Brome
Abraham and Isaac (c. 1450-75)
The York
Crucifixion (c. 1430-40)

Western drama as we know and practise it is virtually unthinkable without the Greek tragedies and Shakespeare's plays. With their intensity, profundity, beauty and continued relevance to whatever we do and are, they have largely shaped the drama of Europe for five hundred years; and they are simply *there*, whenever a dramatist takes up pen or theatre company goes to work. Medieval religious drama claims our attention for different reasons, which are no less cogent in their own way. First of all, it is the dramatic expression of the Christian part of our heritage, without some knowledge of which historic Europe, its thought and social organisation, its literature, arts and politics, cannot be understood. It developed during the long period of Christian triumph in the West, from the tenth to the sixteenth centuries, and must be thought of as both historical drama and religious celebration. It is historical because the plays are dramatisations of Bible events, and it is religious because it was written and presented first within churches and then, as it developed, wherever else was convenient – street, market-place, great hall – as the central social activity of a religious feast.

The plays were performed at the early summer festival of Corpus Christi, which was instituted in the thirteenth century. The two short plays we present in this series were each items in a succession, or *cycle*, of plays, dramatising the religious history of Man from the Creation to the Last Judgement. To present such a cycle, of thirty to fifty plays, a medieval city made a huge social effort, as the York Records, which survive, show. The Church probably originated, and certainly approved, the play-scripts, as well as exercising general religious supervision; the civic authority, in concert with the Church, planned, directed and financed the whole occasion; and the trade guilds each rehearsed, physically mounted and presented their own plays. Sometimes the trade was peculiarly suited to the play. Shipwrights were naturally responsible for Noah plays; the Chester *Abraham and Isaac* was performed by the Barbers (who were also blood-letters and surgeons), and the York *Crucifixion* by the Pinners (nail-makers). It seems that the same men played the same parts year after year: at any rate, there were few rehearsals, and in some late medieval illustrations a man with a book and a sort of conductor's baton – obviously a combined director and prompter – can be seen among the actors. During the sixteenth century, partly as a consequence of the Reformation, the theatre gradually became secularised and professional, and today the only survival of anything like medieval drama, apart from revivals, is at Oberammergau, where a Passion Play is put on by the villagers every ten years.

So medieval drama was a community activity, with its place in the year-rhythm of a whole population. As such it attracted, and expressed, diverse elements of common life. In dramatic terms that we recognise, it contained conflict of realistic character, suspense, pathos and humour, in imaginative renderings and expansions of the Biblical and Bible-related originals. But it also drew on popular entertainment: on mime, acrobatics, song, dance and music and especially on folk drama, with its conventions of slapstick and slaughter, romance and ritual. And it reflected social activities such as processions and disguisings, fighting techniques such as wrestling and weapon-play, games, junketing and horseplay.

Above all, drama was a religious teaching instrument. It showed people, in a directed emotional focus, the chief events in the history of their religion; it gave them dramatic interpretation of holy writ for the strengthening of their faith. *Abraham and Isaac* and the *Crucifixion* were chosen for this series because, besides being fine representative plays, they are related to each other. The medieval Church taught Old Testament events as prefiguring specifically Christian events. So Abraham is God, sacrificing his Son; Isaac is Christ, willingly going to sacrifice in order to redeem Man from sin; Isaac saved is the resurrected Christ, rejoicing in Man's redemption. No wonder that six different medieval *Abraham and Isaac* plays survive. The *Crucifixion* is the central event prefigured in the story, and both in the text and in the television performances the significance of the one play for the other is brought out.

A director must follow the lead given him by Isaac who, as his father prepares to cut off his head, says the words of Christ on the cross: 'Lord, receive me into thy hand!' So Isaac carries a cross-shaped bundle of faggots, just as he does in a thirteenth-century stained-glass window in Canterbury Cathedral; and when the ram appears, the withered thicket by

Isaac (Gary Carp) pleads with his father not to kill him.

the place of sacrifice becomes a green bush sprouting roses (symbols of Christ's Passion). These are clear examples of a kind of cross-reference with which people today may not be familiar. But the director's main means of emphasising parallels between the two plays are in the sets and lighting. The sets are recognisably the same – a rocky, hilltop place of sacrifice. An effect of hard desert light is achieved by lighting mainly from one angle only. The same kind of darkness descends at the moment God appears during Abraham's sacrifice of the ram as descends on the Crucifixion; and the same sort of vivid colour effects are used in both plays at moments of supernatural impact – God appears in a bright red ball in the Old Testament play, and both Isaac saved and Christ crucified appear against deep blue. The combination of deep colours and white light often achieves an effect like stained glass. In sound, the same thunderclap effect is used to herald both God's appearance to Abraham and Isaac, and the moment when the sixth hour had come and 'there was darkness over the whole land' (*Mark* xiv, 33).

As handed down the ages, however, plays are words for speaking and acting to; and medieval plays present us with intricate verse in a language we recognise as our own, though the pronunciation is different and there are many strange words. We decided to use fifteenth-century language and pronunciation, because altering either the form or sound of the dialogue would destroy rhyme and rhythm, lose tone and atmosphere, and lead to actual loss of meaning. The actors, having been instructed in fifteenth-century northern pronunciation (with an East Anglian variant for the Brome play) by Meg Twycross, lecturer in English at the University of Lancaster, found the dialogue, especially of the York play, so concrete and full of suggested action that they freely built on it, with powerful dramatic effects on the performance. This is just as well, since the language of the York play, being mainly fourteenth-century, is so much harder to understand than that of the Brome play, which is of the late fifteenth century. Two of the actors came from Yorkshire and thought they recognised a local style of joking about lazy workmen.

Listening to the dialogue of these plays is therefore rather easier than listening to the dialogue of, say, a film in a foreign language that you know slightly. So you sharpen your eyes to receive the full visual impact and, as far as the words are concerned, concentrate on pitch, tone, facial expression and accompanying action rather than the meaning of every word. It is surprising how much of that York speech you will understand, even though you do it mainly through the range of voice and the action.

The plays are set and costumed in the Biblical times with which their events have made us familiar: *Abraham and Isaac* in the desert world of the Patriarchs (*c.* 2000 BC), the Crucifixion in Roman times. To simulate medieval conventions, with Abraham as a sort of bejewelled Saracen for example, would have meant putting barren historicism before dramatic reality.

The power of these plays lies in the naturalistic action and passion with which familiar Biblical narratives are enacted by recognisably human beings. Amazingly, the intricate stanzas of the poets accommodate natural-sounding speech. But they have another power too. They

Abraham and Isaac preparing to set out for the sacrifice.

can lift the drama at moments of divine manifestation to a pitch of magical dignity. God's promise to Abraham, and Christ's two speeches in the Crucifixion, which are verse paraphrases of parts of the liturgy, succeed superbly. The last phrase of 'Father, forgive them, for they know not what they do' can be recognised in the masterly economy of 'what they work, wot they nought'.

Abraham and Isaac succeeds because father and son in this unnatural predicament are so concretely drawn. Abraham is patriarchal, prophetic and vulnerable: Daniel Massey at the start marvellously shows the transition from Abraham's exhilarated awareness of the divine presence to his glazed fear and dread at the command that he kill his child. Isaac's portrayal is faithful to the medieval literary tradition of the innocent child, the best-known example of which today is Chaucer's 'litel clergeon [choir-boy], seven yeer of age' in the grisly Prioress's Tale. But the little chap in this play, rendered by Gary Carp, is less idealised than Chaucer's: he is dependent on his mother, to whom he several times refers in utmost pathos when thinking about the death he must face. And he takes unreflecting delight in telling the ram how glad he is about the exchange of sacrifice.

The four soldiers in the York *Crucifixion*, who were given names in rehearsal instead of the bald numbers in the manuscript, form a team of negligent but purposeful torturers, who behave in a way that still today illuminates the mentality and method of violent oppression. There is the sergeant, authoritarian and lazy, standing back and enjoying Christ's pain with a deadpan, inquisitive intelligence: the moments when the soldiers make him share the weight-lifting, and when he turns the tables on them by bagging the loot of Christ's 'coat' at the end, are grim comedy. There is Oswald, a more sensitive and neurotic type, the only one who seems to understand the significance of the work he is doing: through his sadistic reaction we feel the nails going into Christ's flesh. There is Thomas, the old soldier, massive-framed and brutal, the 'heavy' whose face, at such moments as when the cross with Christ on it is dropped into the mortise, gives us both victim's pain and torturer's delight. And there is Nicholas, young and skittish, who flits back and forth from Christ to his more staid fellows; an adept in cruelty, infinitely corruptible. All the soldiers, after moments of violent satisfaction, turn casually to the next bit of the job in hand. Against those four, Christ is relaxed and composed except at moments of pain, smiling at the soldiers before lying on the cross to be tied and nailed, and always tranquilly in touch with God – an extraordinary acting feat by John Moreno.

The three soldiers, George Little, Declan Mulholland (wearing helmet) and Ian Oliver (dozing) before setting up the Cross.

The Venetian Twins by Carlo Goldoni
Translated by Frederick Davies
The programme is a shortened version of the play omitting the sub-plot concerning the jewels and telescoping the action surrounding Zanetto's death.

The Twins	Donal Donnelly
Rosaura	Amanda Barrie
Florindo	Jonathan Cecil
Beatrice	Jacqueline Pearce
Lelio	Neil Cunningham
Pancrazio	Milton Johns
Dr Balanzoni	John Evitts
Arlecchino	David Wood
Colombina	Judith Fielding
Brighella	Chris Sullivan
Porter	Kenneth Waller
Music	Dudley Simpson
Designer	David Hitchcock
Director	Paul Kafno

Illustration: *Colombina, Tonino (The wise Twin), Lelio, Rosaura and Beatrice.*

Carlo Goldoni
The Venetian Twins (1748)

From some two hundred years before Christ to the middle of the eighteenth century, Europe, and especially Italy and France, enjoyed a tradition of vigorous comedy – a popular comedy of intrigue verging at times on farce – which appealed to all sections of society. Firmly grounded in real social relationships, this comic mode brought into confrontation master with servant, lover with mistress, scheming old men with marriageable young women, fortune-hunting girls and their avaricious fathers with young men of wealth and standing. However flamboyant and mannered, this drama was fundamentally concerned with the hard realities of passion and social advancement. In Italy, this classical tradition gave rise in post-Renaissance times to an exuberantly funny sort of play.

The Venetian Twins comes at the end of this long line of comic invention. It largely depends for its enchanting sense of pure theatre on the conventions of the *commedia dell'arte*. Carlo Goldoni's romp belongs clearly to a world of 'play', an exotic, artificial world where characters of charm, stupidity or guile are swept along on a mounting tide of implausible predicaments occasioned by the confusing presence of identical twins. The audience is beguiled not so much by their plight, as by the speed and skill with which the dramatic threads are humorously interwoven and finally untangled.

The *commedia dell'arte* tradition on which this play draws heavily was a type of improvised drama popular throughout Italy from the middle of the sixteenth century. Itinerant bands of professional actors delighted local audiences in city or village with improvisations on comic plots. There was no play script or written dialogue, but a scenario giving a basic outline of comic motivation and action on which the players elaborated. They brought these skeletal plays to life with spontaneous dialogue, amusing antics, mime, dance movement, appropriate 'business' and hilarious tumbling and clowning. This strictly non-literary art, which required all-round performers, much as the old music-hall needed versatile song-and-dance artists, appealed to Goldoni whose early plays resembled *commedia dell'arte* scenarios. Much depended on the individual talents of actors, who shaped and guided the loosely-structured dramatic idea, and Goldoni (1707–93) created roles for star members of the acting fraternity in several of his plays, including *The Venetian Twins*.

Essential to *commedia dell'arte* was a cast of stock characters such as Pantaloon, Columbine, Harlequin, Doctor, Captain, Lovers and Intriguing Servants, each of whom was distinguished by easily recognisable costume and a special stage manner. Colombina and Arlecchino, who late in the tradition became lovers (as in this play), were servants; such gay, impertinent, 'low comedy' characters linked and promoted the complications of the plot. Among the middle-class characters, the Doctor was traditionally a black-robed pedant or lawyer, Pantaloon a prosperous merchant in scarlet doublet and hose, and the Captain a pseudo-elegant swashbuckler. All wore masks, or rather dominoes, which covered eyes and nose and so emphasised their role stereotypes. However, as in *The Venetian Twins*, the centre of the stage belonged by custom to the Lovers, who were freer to discover a personal style of their own, although they were subject to the vagaries of a fast-moving plot. Each actor specialised in one particular part which suited his personality and acting ability. Over the years he would develop the character, adding to and changing his material. No two performances were ever alike, for the mood of the moment, the varying expectation and response of audiences, and accidents of improvisation, all ensured constant variety.

With his sure touch for the dramatic mould in which he was working, the mainspring of which was often the theme of confused identity, Goldoni unerringly portrayed the human motives behind the light-hearted façade: young women ensuring their future in terms of men and fortune, young men trying to get women into bed, old men keeping their power when they have lost their potency, and all ranks exploiting their social position and role.

The television production underlines the artificiality of the play form by rigorous avoidance of a natural-looking set. The director draws attention to the cardboard quality of his deliberately theatrical setting by using scenery on which is painted, in careful perspective, a complete Italian street, with house, garden, formal gateway and adjoining inn, while a knowing human sun smiles from the backcloth. In this decorated setting the characters group and move according to a developing pattern as in a complex dance. Rosaura, as played by Amanda Barrie, is a deliciously pretty creature of pouting whims and naïve vanity. The prospect of a man, a marriage and a fortune puts her in a flutter; finger-tips, eyelashes, dangling ear-rings and an escaping curl all tremble in token of her dizzy, innocent femininity. Crashing in upon this pink-and-white

Rosaura (Amanda Barrie).

Donal Donnelly as Zanetto, the foolish Twin.

loveliness comes the boorish, hot-headed Zanetto, the foolish twin whose thoughts are on 'consummation' rather than marriage ceremony, and who is surprised when he gets slapped for forcing himself upon her. He has hardly left the stage when he is replaced by his elegant and manly twin Tonino – two contrasting parts played with joyous virtuosity by Donal Donnelly. Tonino is in love with Beatrice who has run away from home in order to marry him. Around these pairs of lovers gravitate beautifully costumed interferers – Pancrazio, the elderly and hypocritical admirer of Rosaura; Florindo, beau and false friend of Tonino, who has fallen for Beatrice; and Lelio, a braggart dandy unskilled with tongue and sword. All of them, resplendent in peacock and turquoise brocade, claret-coloured and dark green velvet and figured satins of gold, red, pink and emerald, intrigue or duel to gain their desires; inter-mittently in the background fusses the black-clad figure of Rosaura's father, Doctor Balanzoni, whose house is seen in the stage set. Colom-bina and Arlecchino serve their superiors with knowing aplomb – and

David Wood and Judith Fielding as Arlecchino and Colombina.

in so doing, realise their own plans too. Their harlequin colours and pierrot-like make-up suggest pantomine, and indeed their matching costumes of purple, red and white lozenges link them together long before they are united in a marriage contract.

The outstanding difficulty for the playwright lay in the conclusion, when spectators would expect to see both pairs of lovers reconciled. How could Goldoni account for the appearance of only one twin at the end? In the event he avoided the impasse by having the jealous Pancrazio press poison upon Zanetto when the apparently spurned lover is disillusioned with womankind. The 'murderer' is then himself unmasked. These two episodes, which call upon the whole cast to evince personal and social reactions, are expressed by the inspired idea of playing them in dumb-show – with appropriate acrobatic or balletic movements – and at exactly double speed. So the comicality of it all triumphs with Rosaura finding a husband in Lelio, now happily rich, and Beatrice and Tonino comprehensively united.

The Way of the World by William Congreve
The programme concentrates on the central relationships in the play and is mainly made up of scenes from Acts II and III with a curtailed version of the ending.

Mrs Millamant	Francesca Annis
Mr Mirabell	Anthony Ainley
Mrs Marwood	Ann Bell
Mrs Fainall	Petra Davies
Mr Fainall	Neil Stacy
Lady Wishfort	Mary Wimbush
Foible	Jo Kendall
Mincing	Margo Cooper
Sir Wilfull Witwoud	John Savident
Designer	Dacre Punt
Director	John Selwyn Gilbert

Illustration: *Anthony Ainley and Francesca Annis as Mirabell and Mrs Millamant.*

William Congreve
The Way of the World (1700)

In English comedy, only one play by Oscar Wilde, *The Importance of Being Earnest* (1895), and several by George Bernard Shaw (1856–1950) can offer anything like the continual verbal glitter of *The Way of the World*. Wilde was irresponsibly guying the absurdities of upper-class ideas and manners; Shaw, an original reformer, was examining serious moral, social and political issues through a witty and often funny dialectic; but William Congreve (1670–1729) was expressing his own fascination and delight in the way of life of fashionable London society in his own day. His satire, which is mainly conventional, is contained within that frame, and his moral programme is flimsy. In *The Way of the World* everyone intrigues and if, to bring his lovers together in a happy ending, Congreve makes the least objectionable intrigues succeed, there is nothing particularly moral about that except that love, if the playwright can convince the audience of its genuineness, is by comedy's conventions an absolute virtue.

The London society that gave Congreve its stage was dependent on the court of Charles II, whose triumphant return from exile in 1660 on the collapse of the Commonwealth brought a strong reaction against everything associated with the word 'Puritan'. The returned aristocrats and their followers celebrated liberation with a licence which was expressed in the arts of the age, even in the public art of drama. Yet Restoration drama was comparatively private, because only fashionable society went to the theatre; the 'respectable' middle classes remained as hostile as they had been ever since the rise of Puritanism in Shakespeare's time, and largely declined to attend. Hence from 1660 to 1700 there were never more than two theatres open in London. Not surprisingly, in the long succeeding period during which middle-class ideals determined public taste, Restoration comedy was thought too indecent to stage, and it was not until the 1920s that plays by Congreve and his contemporaries such as Wycherley, Etherege, Vanbrugh and Farquhar began to be revived.

But of course indecency, that boringly legalistic concept, does not explain the popularity of the play, though it contributes something. Livers of the seamy life, whether in baronial halls and city banqueting rooms, or dockside pubs and country fairs, often display an honesty about the various facts of life, and an urgency to gratify secret and anti-social desires, which are positively funny. No vice, no comic satire. The rakes and wantons whose life Restoration dramatists so lovingly chronicled were too intent on practising pleasure to be able to conceal their preoccupations.

Every name in this kind of drama carries its meaning: Mirabell is 'admirable', Millamant is loved by the thousand, Mrs Marwood tries to upset other people's plans, and Lady Wishfort is a raddled matron

The identification line-up (l. to r.): Millamant, Sir Wilfull Witwoud, Mrs Marwood, Fainall, Mrs Fainall, Mincing, Foible, Lady Wishfort, Mirabell.

starved of a beau's attentions. This naming of characters by their most prominent qualities came from the old Comedy of Humours, in which characterisation was achieved by basing everything a person said or did on a single trait or 'humour'. Like the *commedia dell'arte*, which based characters on roles or stations in life, the Comedy of Humours was based on types. Just as *The Venetian Twins* is a late variant of *commedia dell'arte*, so *The Way of the World* represents a development of the Comedy of Humours. Its people, if they are indeed partly 'humours', are also as humanly complex as they need to be to fulfil their roles in their hothouse setting.

The television programme presents parts of the last four acts of *The Way of the World*, and concentrates on the efforts of Mirabell to win the hand and fortune of Millamant. To do this he must propitiate Millamant's aunt, Lady Wishfort, who controls Millamant's fortune and regards Mirabell as an enemy because he once pretended to love her. He does it in part by saving the fortune of Lady Wishfort's daughter, Mrs Fainall, his former mistress whom he had married off to someone else when he had thought her pregnant. Such a naked summary by no means covers all the bewildering details of the various intrigues, which embrace a Welsh maid, a titled country bumpkin, a sophisticated fortune-hunter (Fainall) and a third beauty, Mrs Marwood, the lover of Fainall. One of the spices of the play is that all the women just named have been, or are, in love with Mirabell.

In spite of the aristocratic ambience suggested by the titles in the list of characters, such a plot, rooted in sex-pursuit and money-chasing cruder than those in *The Venetian Twins*, might well evoke a tawdry milieu, with fleas and soiled shirts amid the glitter. But there is the language: musical and exquisitely phrased, and sparkling with witticisms which would be as arresting if isolated in an anthology of wit as they are in the dramatic context of the play. This production lets the language rule the style of presentation. The set is chastely harmonious, in pink and silver gilt with a black-and-white chequered floor, and the costumes and furnishings opulently suggest the period.

The play is memorable for a number of scenes of a kind traditional in English and French seventeenth-century comedy. There is the opening scene of this production, in which Mrs Fainall and Mrs Marwood reveal their longings for love while professing hatred of men:

Mrs Fainall: ... While they are lovers, if they have fire and spirit, their jealousies are insupportable. And when they cease to love, they loathe.

Mrs Marwood: But say what you will, 'tis better to be left than never to have been loved. To refuse the sweets of life because they once must leave us, is as preposterous as to wish to have been born old.

There is the scene in which Lady Wishfort makes her toilet in anticipation of being wooed by Sir Rowland, Mirabell's fictitious uncle. Mary Wimbush, in a strong and deeply felt performance, finds something endearingly girlish in the feather-brained harridan, and brings out her fundamental honesty as well, so that one is moved even while laughing at her:

Foible: Your ladyship has frowned a little too rashly, indeed, madam. There are some cracks discernible in the white varnish.

Lady Wishfort: Let me see the glass. Cracks, say'st thou? Why I am arrantly flayed; I look like an old peeled wall.

Lady Wishfort (Mary Wimbush) at toilet, with Foible.

Most famous of all, partly because it grants the audience its dearest
wish – that Mirabell and Millamant become engaged – and partly
because of the exquisite balance between the two characters, who reveal
themselves as passionate and idealistic about love under their formal cor-
rectness of behaviour, is the proviso scene. It is the best known of the
many proviso scenes, in which lovers state their conditions before agree-
ing to marry, that were staged during the period:

Millamant: ... But let us be very strange and well-bred; let us be
as strange as if we had been married a great while, and
as well-bred as if we were not married at all.

Towards the end of the scene, Mirabell makes the proviso that Millamant shall not try to conceal pregnancy by 'strait-lacing, squeezing for
a shape, till you mould my boy's head like a sugar loaf,' and their shared
contemplation of 'breeding' and its necessary preliminary 'endeavours'
is exquisitely sensual:

Mirabell: ... Item, when you shall be breeding –
Millamant: Ah! Name it not.
Mirabell: – which may be presumed as a blessing on our
endeavours –
Millamant: Odious endeavours!

The scene beautifully resolves the war between the sexes which has been
simmering and bubbling throughout the play.

In this production, since only part of the play is presented, the
emphasis happens to fall on the women, and perhaps it is on Millamant,
the fullest and most original character, that we should leave the lime-
light. She justifies Mirabell's comparison of her to a whirlwind, in her
capricious mastery of social exchanges and her hectic but graceful eventual submission. Francesca Annis makes the most memorable moment
when Mirabell leaves her at the end of the proviso scene; she gazes after
him besotted, with swimming eyes, not even hearing what Mrs Fainall
is saying.

Ubu Roi by Alfred Jarry
Translated by Cyril Connolly and Simon Watson Taylor
A condensed version of the whole play.

Ubu Roi	Donald Pleasance
Ma Ubu	Brenda Bruce
Captain Macnure	Neil Cunningham
King Wenceslas	John Evitts
Boggerlas	Oengus Macnamara
Gyron	Christopher Asante
Heads	Bunny Reed
Tails	Paul Toothill
Queen Rosamund	Jaqueline Delhaye
Other parts	Glen Cunningham
	Roger Neil
	Michael Cullen
	Basil Clarke
	Gerald Moon
Designer	Dacre Punt
Director	Paul Kafno

Illustration: *Donald Pleasence and Brenda Bruce as Pa and Ma Ubu after the seizure of the crown of Poland.*

Alfred Jarry
Ubu Roi (1896)

Alfred Jarry's *Ubu Roi* is an iconoclastic stage cartoon, which seems to read like an inconsequential schoolboy rag dependent on crude slapstick and lavatory humour. But in performance it turns out to be an exuberantly savage burlesque, not only of all sorts of historic theatre conventions, but of the worlds of morality and politics. Since the targets of its satire are still with us, and since its many modes vary from scene to scene and sometimes even from speech to speech, the play attracts the spirit of comic invention in any age. The continuing relevance of its discerning frivolity is widely accepted, and directors usually bring to it contemporary techniques as well as incorporating allusions to contemporary events in their interpretation.

Eighty years ago in Paris the famous opening word of the play rang out in the theatre for the first time: 'Merdre!' That is, the French word which is exactly equivalent to our expletive 'Shit!', plus a final 'r'; it is translated by Cyril Connolly in our version as 'Pschitt' – a happy invention. The star actor from the Comédie Française who in 1896 delivered the word like a 'hammer-blow' had difficulty in finding the right voice and manner for the part. The director, Lugné-Poe of the Théâtre de l'Oeuvre, originally confessed of the play that he 'didn't know which way to take hold of the thing'. His ultimate advice to his leading man was to imitate the author's own speech and strange, stiff gestures, for Alfred Jarry (1873–1907) – twenty-three-year-old *enfant terrible* of French letters, friend of poets and painters, anarchic and almost dwarf-sized rebel – lived, ate and slept Ubu and knew exactly how he wanted his play performed. He saw it as *guignol*, slapstick. The Punch-and-Judy element was in his mind when he advocated a mask for the hero and he recommended that there should be no scene changes, but a simple backdrop; an actor should walk on with a placard indicating each new scene; a cardboard horse's head should be hung round Ubu's neck in the equestrian episodes; shoddy, modern costumes should be worn 'to make the play even more wretched and horrible'.

The original version of *Ubu Roi* was written when Jarry was fifteen, and produced as a puppet play in the family attic. It was not entirely his own composition but the joint achievement of himself and several schoolfellows at the lycée in Rennes. The favourite sport of this precocious gang was to bait their fat physics master, Monsieur Hébert (variously known as Père Heb, Hébé, Ebé, etc.): they made him the pot-bellied hero of cruel little sketches, in which everything they studied from Shakespeare to mathematics was cleverly burlesqued. Schoolboy humour it certainly was, but savage at times, and Jarry in particular brought prodigious reading and learning to the enterprise.

Unlike most young raggers Jarry did not lose interest in his subject after leaving school. With his sense of the ridiculous and his satiric imagination, he went on developing the saga of Père Hébé. He adopted an even more ludicrous name for his petty dictator, and elevated him to kingship: 'Ubu Roi'. By the time the play reached the stage, eight years after its first performance as a puppet play, its royal hero had become a cartoon monster of violence and terror on a European scale: in the television production, the two syllables of his name are turned into a rallying cry with the horrifying power that 'Heil Hitler' has in the continent that produced gas chambers. The grotesque mythical figure that was to haunt the modern stage had arrived: a cowardly, gluttonous nincompoop who, egged on by his wife, murders and replaces the King of Poland and then tyrannises and slaughters all who stand in his path – nobles, judges, financiers and peasants; imprisons his chief supporter; conducts a reign of terror at home and abroad which ends only with his fall; and then sails away with his confidence undiminished.

Turn-of-the-century opinion saw in this monstrous buffoon a 'terrifying image of the animal nature of man, his cruelty and ruthlessness'. Twentieth-century critics, in the light of two world wars, see *Ubu Roi* as in some sense prophetic of the holocaust which was to come; the barbarism and megalomania of its hero were echoed in reality. The literary world of the late 1890s divided into detractors and supporters of Jarry.

Mallarmé, one of the subtlest poets of his day, said of Ubu: 'He enters into the repertoire of high taste and haunts me.' Yeats also sensed Jarry's importance and foresaw, though regretfully from the point of view of his own generation, the influence that character and creator would come to exert. His famous prophecy, 'After us, the Savage God', has been amply fulfilled in twentieth-century life and art. Innovators themselves, Mallarmé and Yeats saw the significance of Jarry, whose poetic fury synthesised and transformed historical, literary and stage traditions, making a new and distorted vision from them.

When persuading Lugné-Poe to stage the play, Jarry had stressed that his work incorporated a variety of theatrical conventions. His ribald earthiness and simple symbolic devices are like those used in medieval drama and the mummers' plays of folk tradition, and his uncluttered stage derives from the Elizabethan theatre. From neo-classical theatre he took the theme of the hero who fights for his honour, his ambition and his ideals – a convention which, with venomous relish, he turned upside down.

Above all he parodied Shakespeare, to whom he mockingly refers in the superscription to the text. In the very first scene Ma Ubu employs her gross charms, much as Lady Macbeth used her marital position and sexual initiative, to urge her hesitant husband on to murder. The *Macbeth* theme of the temptress-wife comes out in her crude advice:

If I were you I'd try to get that bum on a throne. You could become enormously rich, eat as many bangers as you liked, and roll through the streets in a fine carriage.

The murder plot in *Julius Caesar*, with the meeting of the conspirators, is also parodied. King Wenceslas's queen has premonitions of disaster like those of Calpurnia before Caesar's departure for the Capitol, and her fears are confirmed by the same kind of ritualised murder. In Jarry's travesty Wenceslas dies whimpering, 'Help! Help! Help! Holy Virgin, I'm dying!', and Ubu leaves the scene of murder gleeful and unrepentant: 'Ha! I have the crown. Now for the others!'

The television director has interpreted this mock-heroic extravaganza in contemporary ways, using some of the techniques which have been developed in cinema and television for presenting caricature and farce. Comic routines used by Laurel and Hardy, the Marx Brothers and the Crazy Gang are echoed, and one is reminded at times of Monty Python and the Goodies. In the shortening of the play for this series, some of the Rabelaisian linguistic invention is lost, but the original concentration of Jarry on the brute mechanics of the plot has accordingly been reinforced.

In the hands of Donald Pleasance, who gives a consistently low-keyed performance which is all the more chilling for that, Ubu evokes Groucho Marx with his childlike lack of scruple and blinkered self-importance; but the unimaginative matter-of-factness of brutality and greed is always there. Brenda Bruce's Ma Ubu is more various, as the text demands. Her artificially inflated voluptuousness bubbling over a sheath of sizzling pink, she scolds, cajoles, flounces and writhes her way through the play – blonde barmaid, gangster's moll, femme fatale, gracious duchess or the Archangel Gabriel as occasion demands.

Our first sight of the couple is as two puppet replicas gesturing in a Punch and Judy booth. The scene widens to show that this is an image on a television screen being watched by Pa and Ma Ubu themselves, sitting in armchairs in a setting like a fairground, with neon and plastic and flashing coloured lights, and grotesque heads overpeering. Once Ma Ubu has planted in Ubu's mind the idea of murdering the king she provides a feast for the intended conspirators, at which two items on the menu are a revolting-looking dish of parsons' noses and cauliflower à la pshitt. This of course develops into a slapstick food-throwing scene. Having gained the support of Captain Macnure (pronounced M'Nure), Ubu turns into a cigar-smoking gangster in order to hatch the murder plot in a sleazy saloon-like interior cluttered with beer cans. Here we meet the black fellow-conspirator Gyron who later cuckolds Ubu.

The murder of Wenceslas has the brutal suddenness of *grand guignol* or circus clowning – Bam! and he is dead. Ubu launches into tyranny, and sends tweed-clad aristocrats in deer-stalkers, red-robed judges, and city gents in morning coats, pin-striped trousers and top hats 'down the hatch' to their deaths. The execution chamber, with its green and metal gleam and its flashing light, comes straight out of a science fiction film. With the nobility and the middle class destroyed, Ubu confronts in their own home two discontented and apprehensive peasants who in Jarry's style represent multitudes. Stepping through the door ahead of his henchmen like a clown through a paper hoop, he advances on his extortionately taxed subjects, cigar in mouth, like a king of the Chicago underworld. The episode ends in Marx Brothers style: dancing in jubilation at his mastery of events, Ubu slashes the scenery to shreds with his umbrella while his followers chant 'Oo-boo! Oo-boo!'.

Ubu's run of success ends when he foolishly abandons Captain Macnure, who allies himself with Wenceslas's son and the Russian army.

Ubu, with his henchmen, Heads and Tails, and Gyron,
hectors his peasant subjects.

His usurped crown threatened, Ubu rides off to battle after being
propped up on his pantomime horse, and flourishes his sabre like Henry
V urging his English 'unto the breach'. Ma Ubu, left behind, seduces
Gyron and steals the treasures of Poland. Ubu's battle is shown in puppet
sequence. He escapes with his bodyguard, Heads and Tails, and takes
refuge in a cave in Lithuania which glitters like a setting for Santa Claus
in a big shop. An encounter here with a bear probably owes its invention
to the famous stage direction in Act III of *The Winter's Tale*, 'Exit,
pursued by a bear'. Meanwhile, back in Poland, Gyron has been chopped
in quarters by Boggerlas, and Ma Ubu has escaped the avenging Poles.
She meets Ubu in the cave, and as he begins to beat her for her treachery –
though he does not know of her adultery – the Polish army under Boggerlas arrive. Ubu's party escape and sail for their home in France,
drenched and imperturbable, some of them destined to die of laughing
while on board ship.

Jarry's final implication is presumably that Ubuism is at home in
France. Unfortunately, it remains rife in the world at large, and the
dramatic ways of exposing it are widely spread through documentary
and satiric drama, whether on stage, film or television.

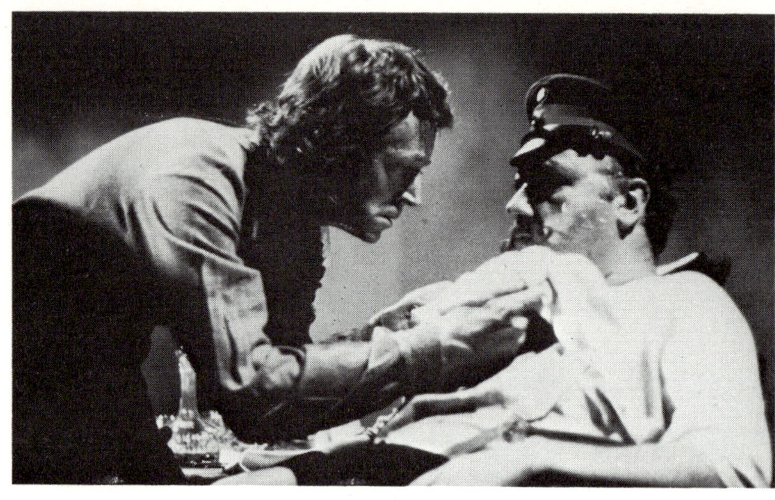

Woyzeck by Georg Büchner
Translated by Victor Price
An original reconstruction of the play, which was left unfinished at the author's death, with a few cuts.

Narrator	David Wood
Woyzeck	David Collings
Marie	Cyd Hayman
Andres	Colin Farrell
Drum Major	David Calder
Captain	John Bryans
Doctor	Peter Copley
Margret	Olwen Griffiths
Sergeant/Jew	Michael da Costa
Old Man/Second Man	Sydney Arnold
First Man	Allan McClelland
Kathe	Susie Blake
Landlord	Cyril Tawney
Designer	David Hitchcock
Director	John Selwyn Gilbert

Illustration: *Woyzeck (David Collings) shaves the Captain (John Bryans).*

Georg Büchner
Woyzeck (1837)

First performed 1913

Georg Büchner (1813–37) died of typhus at the age of twenty-three. In his five years of adult life after entering university he completed his initial medical studies while at the same time writing and working for radical causes so vigorously that he had to leave Germany to avoid arrest. In exile he was recommended for a doctorate on the strength of his anatomical research, and began teaching at the University of Zurich. He translated two plays by Hugo and wrote four of his own, of which three survive.

It took Büchner only five weeks to complete his first play, *Danton's Death*, a spacious and densely written tragedy which successfully fuses profound insight into the hero's complex character with a just but not judging sense of the spirit and events of the French Revolution. In this dramatisation of the trial and death of the sensual realist Danton, whom he makes something of a philosopher (as he himself was), Büchner expresses the same passionate concern for natural life and the same existential despair that are found in his other works, including *Woyzeck*. When studying the French Revolution, Büchner had felt 'annihilated by the brutal inevitability of history'–a phrase which applies as aptly to the inarticulate peasant soldier Woyzeck in his nameless province as to the clever politician dying on the stage centre of Europe.

Woyzeck is based on an actual event. In 1821 a soldier called Woyzeck killed the widow with whom he had been formerly living because she would have sex with other soldiers. At his trial it was suggested that he might be insane, and a Dr Clarus examined him at length. Clarus, whose report in a journal dealing with mental diseases was read by Büchner, concluded that Woyzeck was sane, and in 1824 the murderer was publicly executed in Leipzig. Clarus, secure and 'objective' on his eminence of respectability and privilege, showed no understanding of Woyzeck's down-trodden existence. Büchner crams into the play, which is only twenty-four pages long and contains as many episodic scenes, an entire vision of oppressed and suffering humanity. His Woyzeck, who, unlike the actual, drunken, Woyzeck, is in his dumb way deeply virtuous, is oppressed by society in the persons of the Doctor and the Captain, who exploit and abuse him; by the Drum-Major who seduces Marie, his woman, and then persecutes him; and above all by Marie, whose infidelity destroys the one prop which can hold him up in a hostile and largely incomprehensible world.

Apart from these main characters a number of others, unnamed except in their function, give to Woyzeck's tragedy, by their comments and action, not just the background of a real society but a spacious feeling of an ironic, conspiratorial universe. There is Woyzeck's and Marie's child (a baby in this production), who roots Woyzeck's being in the promise of budding life, and expresses his love for Marie. There is Andres, his friend, who is an essential character because he is the only person to whom Woyzeck can communicate his bewildered musings when not under hostile pressure; and it is to Andres that, movingly, Woyzeck gives his few possessions when he has decided to kill Marie. There are the two apprentices (elderly medical students in this production), first brawling and talking about money, and then mocking religion in despair. There is the Jew who sells Woyzeck the murder knife. There is Kathe, in whom he hopes to drown his sorrows after killing Marie, but who sees the blood on his sleeve and so ends his hopes of escaping justice. There is the Landlord of the tavern of that scene, and of the earlier one in which the Drum-Major and Marie dance and flirt, watched by Woyzeck. And most important of all these, there is the Showman, who demonstrates in his patter that man is no more and no less a piece of nature than his own fairground horse which 'drops a little visiting card'. In this production, the Showman also acts as a compère, announcing the scenes of the different episodes and thus enhancing the ironic tone in a Brechtian manner.

Woyzeck has been called the first modern tragedy, because it has a working-class hero whose predicament is portrayed with insight and compassion and two middle-class characters, the Doctor and the Captain, who are presented as cruel grotesques. But its importance is much greater than that. In its poetic vision, its scale, variety and scope of theme, it anticipates many of the major achievements of modern drama – and 'modern drama' is thought of as beginning in the last quarter of the nineteenth century, fifty years after *Woyzeck* was written. In its psychological perceptions, it also anticipates Freud: the Captain, the Doctor, Marie and even the Drum-Major can be discussed as precursors of psychoanalytical symbolism. They are 'cases' in whom we recognise types of behaviour which are widely found.

The poetic vision of the play is communicated above all by the language and here the translation, however correct and tasteful, has an English tone of its own which softens the impact of the original. The play was written in Hessian dialect accompanied by folk-songs, and so has the kind of tone and atmosphere that we might associate with, say, the Border Ballads. The translation and the avoidance of standard pronunciation by all the actors except those playing the Doctor and the Captain enable something of the original force to be caught. The language, spoken as dialect, can encompass the diversity of dramatic situation and register Büchner required.

In the very first scene, in the misty wood where Woyzeck and Andres are cutting sticks, a ghostly atmosphere is created by a mixture of speech and song. Woyzeck expresses his night fears, and through them his dread of fate:

Do you see that light patch on the grass over there? Where the toadstools are. That's where the head comes rolling down every night ... It was the freemasons, Andres.

And the song of Andres follows:

> A pair of hares were sitting there
> Nibbling the green green grass.

Büchner would know the occult traditions about the hare, bringer of bad luck. There is something Shakespearian about the breadth of vision in that scene, and its easy transition from mode to mode, which sets the tone and foreshadows the scale of the whole play.

The universal scale of the drama easily accommodates a number of references to the Bible, the influence of which is powerfully felt by both Woyzeck and his Marie. Woyzeck expresses its supernatural and apocalyptic force more than once, as when he gives Marie some idea of his night experience:

Doesn't the good book say: 'And behold, there was a smoke coming from the land like the smoke of an oven'?
And when the Captain, whom he is shaving in order to earn a few extra pence, accuses him of immorality in having fathered an illegitimate child, Woyzeck confuses him by quoting, 'Suffer little children to come unto me'. Then Marie passionately identifies with the Woman Taken in Adultery, but knows she is incapable of following her example of reform, because it is in her own nature to be a whore. As Woyzeck ponders her infidelity there is something almost Hamlet-like in his confused attempt to reconcile the appearance and the reality of another human being:
No: it would show on you. Every man is a chasm; you get dizzy when you look down. Suppose it was true. She walks like innocence itself.

But for all the moral intensity Woyzeck expresses in moments like that, his life is dominated by cruder factors of fate and necessity. Every person except Andres, every circumstance, bears on him with brutal weight: the carnal needs of Marie and the Drum Major, the pseudo-scientific needs of the Doctor, the need of the Captain to be comforted and reinforced in his sense of his own superiority, society's impersonal condemnation of Woyzeck to subsistence-level living, the supernatural hostility of Nature itself. From Woyzeck's point of view, it is a brute creation which is trying to turn him into a brute.

Money is an essential part of this brute creation. It is repeatedly mentioned by many of the characters, and Woyzeck sees the possession of it as passport to the moral life. His need of it drives him to the abasement of acting as a guinea-pig in the experiments of the Doctor, who puts him on a diet of peas, buys his urine and is always taking his pulse and making clinical observations about him. Woyzeck is treated as a brute, but only becomes one when he kills Marie.

The climax is a savage and protracted killing by the pond under a blood-red moon, followed by Woyzeck's grisly return to Marie's corpse in search of the knife; and there is an ironic anti-climax in the last scene, when the soon-to-be-condemned murderer leans fondly over the baby who will be left parentless to fend off the world's cruelty.

The television production is strongly atmospheric. The sweat, heat and sex of the text are fully suggested naturalistically; the soldier's trumpet, whore's reward of earrings, and murderer's knife, become evocative images; the songs are movingly sung; and the stark poetry of the dialogue is given full value. David Collings plays a haunted and bewildered Woyzeck who stays in the mind, and in the scenes with the Captain

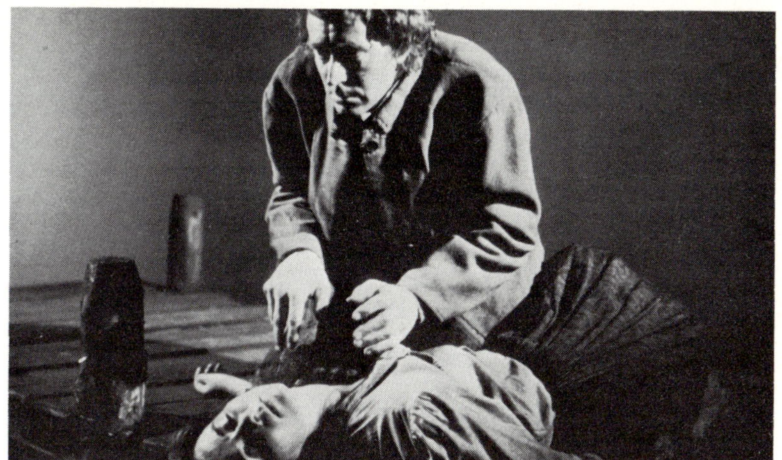

Woyzeck after the murder of Marie (Cyd Hayman).

and the Doctor he achieves a memorable pathos by studied underplaying. John Bryans exactly catches the Captain's peculiar cruelty and frightened emptiness masquerading as high-principled self-confidence: the camera, shooting him from in front and below as he is shaved, raises him to a threatening yet comic eminence. Peter Copley's Doctor, preoccupied with his own supposed wit and knowledge, is fussily and obtusely cruel to all, even the Captain; and Cyd Hayman lives up to Marie's boast that her 'lips are as red as madame's with her mirrors down to the floor'.

This play is a phenomenon which anticipated by half a century the sordid naturalism and political radicalism of Zola – though deterministic despair rather than reforming zeal gives it its great impact. It also foreshadows the various devices of expressionism which were to become a vogue in Germany fifty years later: episodic scenes succeeding each other with cumulative contrapuntal effect; unusual and often surrealist violence; savagely dislocated dialogue; and nameless characters without realistic depth, each giving one overwhelming impression. But having all these, and binding them poetically to the universal theme of helpless man grappling with inexorable necessity, *Woyzeck* for all its shortness is greater than any play by Zola or a German expressionistic dramatist. *Woyzeck* is best known in the form Alban Berg gave it for his masterpiece, the atonal opera *Wozzeck* (1925), which gives Büchner's play its supreme dramatic expression.

Peer Gynt by Henrik Ibsen
Translated by Michael Meyer
The programme concentrates on Act V when Peer has returned home,
interspersed with short sequences from Acts I–III.

Peer Gynt	Patrick Mower
Strange Passenger/	
Thin Person	Peter Copley
Button Moulder	Kenneth Cranham
Aase	Betty Hardy
Solveig	Lorna Heilbron
Priest	Basil Clarke
Old Man of the Mountains	Esmond Knight
Other Parts	John Wentworth
	Eric Mason
	Billy Hamon
	David Neilson
	Roy Spencer
	Gillian Bailey
Designer	George Wisner
Director	John Selwyn Gilbert

Illustration: *Peer Gynt (Patrick Mower) hopefully greets the Thin Person (Peter Copley).*

Henrik Ibsen
Peer Gynt (1867)

Henrik Ibsen (1828–1906) is the only dramatist represented in this series by two plays. This is not just because he is the undisputed master of modern drama, but because the range of his work requires that two different kinds of play are presented. Both *Peer Gynt* and the group of plays which includes *The Wild Duck* (1884) have deeply influenced modern and contemporary theatre; and Ibsen's world in both is, in essence, one that even today we recognise as our own. That is why we acknowledge him as the first great modern dramatist.

Peer Gynt is a poetic epic play in thirty-eight scenes which is set not only in twenty different places in Norway, but also at sea and in various places in Africa. It belongs in form to the nineteenth-century romantic tradition of grand verse drama which produced Goethe's *Faust*: there are aspects of Peer which remind one of both Goethe's Faust and Marlowe's Doctor Faustus: all three heroes see their aspirations, their desires and even their sins in a cosmic perspective.

The play is, in fact, a poem in various lyrical metres with short rhyming lines, and was not intended for the stage. But seven years after writing it, when it had become popular through reading, Ibsen decided to have it staged and commissioned Grieg to write music for it. It was accordingly put on in Oslo in 1876 with grand musical effects, with many of the more discursive scenes severely shortened and those which did not lend themselves to music (such as the scene on the capsized dinghy) cut out altogether. In spite of containing elements which clearly

Peer saves himself after the shipwreck at the expense of the Cook (Billy Hamon).

satirised Norwegian people and movements, it was an instant success and was soon performed in many European countries, though not in England until 1911.

Peer Gynt was the name of an actual character who had lived about a century before in Gudbrandsdal, a region where Ibsen once conducted research in folk studies. He was famed as a story-teller and congenital liar, but in Ibsen's hands, the character becomes an imaginative, self-indulgent young man, a hedonist who always recognises the good and the ideal, but fecklessly and self-analytically falls for the bad and for the compromise, and yet expects his soul to enter a snug haven at the last—a really modern, not to say contemporary, anti-hero. Through Peer's attitudes, and through the attitudes of people whom he meets during the play, Ibsen attacked aspects of Norwegian life that he disliked: the cowardice (as he saw it) which prevented Norway going to the help of her neighbour when Denmark was invaded by Prussia in 1864; her insularity and chauvinism; the vapidity of her provincial life; her religious puritanism; her linguistic obscurantists who wanted to elevate an artificially strengthened country dialect to the status of a national language different from that of Denmark. He also satirised through Peer the characteristics of various people he knew, including himself, and modelled a number of episodes on stories in Norwegian folk-lore.

In fact, Ibsen thought that Peer Gynt would arouse interest only in Norway. Apart from Act IV which is set in Africa and deals with the middle-aged Peer's gratification of uncommitted self and his eventual disillusionment and collapse, the sense of place in the play is powerfully Norwegian. Although there is virtually no description of nature – which in any case would both read and perform undramatically – yet in almost every scene in Norway aspects of the country, its life, natural qualities and climate, are alluded to or evoked. Mountain and crag, moor and bog, pine forest and lake, animals and birds of this wild habitat, provide the environment for the scenes and crop up repeatedly in the verse. The life of the nestling valley villages, threatened by flood or avalanche, appears in wedding and funeral and auction scenes, and the fifth act starts with storm at sea and shipwreck on the rocky coast. The atmosphere is always defined – clear night-heaven with close-sparkling stars, or snowpeaks at sunset, or bewildering and suffocating mists, or storm threatening. And yet, not long after its first performance in Norway, *Peer Gynt* began to be translated into other languages, and its fame spread

Peer is struck by the beauty of Solveig (Lorna Heilbron) at a wedding.

from country to country, with each new audience finding it directly relevant to their own national qualities and predicaments.

But if *Peer Gynt* were nothing more than a satire on certain characteristics found in Ibsen's native country at one time in history and likely to be found elsewhere as well, it would hardly have held the imagination of Europe for a hundred years. Its main subject is not the pettinesses of nineteenth-century Norway, but the trouble that fallible man has in making a decent show of his life. Lying in self-aggrandisement, seducing desperate, innocent girls and enjoying sex with loose women, making money in doubtful ways, surviving shipwreck at the expense of others, making almost impossible demands of a loving woman – all are easy. But because Peer does these things in the effort to satisfy his ego and preserve himself, and knows in his heart that they are wrong, he is hunted by the society whose laws he has flouted, and haunted by spectres of his own creating. One of these is the Great Boyg, a formless spirit of gloom and unease who speaks, in this production as in some others, with the voice of Peer himself. The Boyg is something subtler than conscience: it is a voice without substance, which knows what Peer is up to, knows the consequences, and advises him accordingly: 'Go round!' and that is what Peer does: he meets something difficult, some challenge which might bring out a fine kind of self, and instead of making an effort, he dodges the issue, justifying himself as he does so.

When Solveig, the girl whom he really loves and who truly loves him, leaves her family to join him in the snowbound upland forest where he lives as an outlaw, the spectres of his ugliest lascivious adventure – the troll princess and her fast-growing brat by Peer – haunt him. Instead of facing his past with Solveig at his side, he sentimentally imagines he will sully her purity unless he repents and does penance first. He 'goes round' and, asking Solveig to wait for him however long he is away, he leaves her, to return only when he is an old man. We do not see the troll woman in the programme, but we do see her father, the Old Man of the Mountains, who is spookily played by Esmond Knight, near the end of the play. He puts Peer's life in his own perspective, telling him that he has lived like a troll by being an egoist who has lived for himself alone. And 'to be oneself is to kill oneself', as the Button-Moulder, another spirit, this time of retribution, tells him in the next scene.

The Button-Moulder is one of three characters in the last act who are all, in their different ways, ambassadors of death. Together the Strange Passenger, the Thin Person (both played by Peter Copley) and

Peer learns more truths about himself from the Old Man of the Mountains (Esmond Knight).

the Button-Moulder (Kenneth Cranham) give such a supernatural feeling to that whole part of the play about Peer's return to Norway and his last days that, as Michael Meyer suggests, 'we must surely take that fifth Act as representing either the unreeling of his past life in his mind at the moment of death or (which is perhaps the same thing) as the wandering of his soul in purgatory'. The Strange Passenger, whom we see in the shipwreck scenes, terrifies Peer by asking for his corpse and suggesting that if the ship sank, so might Peer: in this play, in which reality and fantasy, conscious and subconscious, are so freely expressed and interwoven, we could take that shipwreck as the occasion of Peer's death. But whether we do or not, the feeling of death, and the sense that Peer is trying both to find out what his life has meant and to justify it to superhuman judges, remain.

The Button-Moulder has a ladle in which he has been instructed by 'the Master' to melt Peer down into nothingness, because he has done nothing bad enough to be condemned to hell-torment or good enough to be given a place in heaven. Peer pleads to be allowed to serve a short time in hell: as an egoist, he cannot bear the thought of being extinguished altogether. The Button-Moulder gives him one more chance, and yet another, to prove that he has been his true self, either for good or evil. Desperately looking for a priest, he thinks he has found one when he comes across the Thin Person, a man in priest's cassock with a fowling-net for catching souls. Peer soon sees his cloven hoof and again begs unavailingly to be taken into hell. The ensuing discussion about Peer's life is the concluding one. When Peer has tricked the Thin Person into leaving him, the Button-Moulder appears for the last time to claim him, but is temporarily frustrated by Solveig's song, because Peer wants to cry out his sins to her as she cradles him. As day dawns on them and the play ends, the second-act verdict of the Great Boyg is confirmed: 'He was too strong. There were women behind him.' This ending, which appears indefinite and hardly a rounding-off of dramatic arguments advanced earlier, is puzzling, because one would expect there to be a positive conclusion, with Peer bound for either heaven or hell or, failing both, for the Button-Moulder's ladle. In fact, such a quasi-religious moralistic ending seems to be in view from the beginning of the last act, and the whole play, with its mixture of human and allegorical figures, all relating directly to a single central character, seems to be a modern descendant of a medieval morality play – a kind of *Everyman*. Peer often quotes the Bible against himself.

But Ibsen's scope is, if possible, both wider and more modern than that. The arguments of the ambassadors of death and the activity of such folk-myth beings as the trolls, the Great Boyg and the Threadballs, taken all together, do not make a Christian framework. If there is a view implied in the play, it is nearer to a modern existentialist view than to any other. The ruling idea seems to be that for each person there is an appropriate path of self-determination, which can be discovered through making conscious decisions. Most of the allegorical figures can be seen as representatives of Peer's subconscious who are in revolt against him because he fails to become what he wants to be and what, given his nature, he ought to be. The moral aspect of all this – and of course there is one – is incidental to the goal of achieving harmonious self-determination, which cannot be reached in isolation, by thinking of oneself alone. One of the moments at which Peer is nearest to his best self, is when he comforts his dying mother with one of his fantasies.

If Peer is saved at the end – however temporarily – by a woman's love, it is presumably because Ibsen is less interested in following either a religious or a philosophical theory than in expressing a profound and pragmatic view of life. Things are just so. At this stage of his career Ibsen's view is a romantic one, the vision of a young man, but already so complex that *Peer Gynt*, like many of Ibsen's later plays, defies final anlysis. He invokes in it the huge pretensions of the Romantic age. Peer is conceived as a world figure, who sees himself, in his great speech of self-recognition after the Thin Person has left him, as a shooting star:

> We flash for a moment, then our light is quenched
> And we disappear into the void for ever.

With all his faults, he aspires as only a Romantic can, identifying his aspirations and regrets with the controlling cosmic presences:

> Beautiful sun and beautiful earth,
> Why did you bear my mother and give her light?

In essence he is a poet, with a poet's eye for both the beauties of creation and his own miserable failings. He is an authentic person whom we can recognise and understand, and who illuminates our human experience:

> There sail two brown eagles.
> The wild geese fly to the south.
> But I must trudge here and stumble
> Knee-deep in the mire and filth.

With all its ranging in the worlds of reality and fantasy, conscious and subconscious, *Peer Gynt* remains curiously concrete in every scene. The places are real, and so are the characters even if some of them function as abstractions. The television programme accordingly does not emphasise the expressionistic and the supernatural, but gains strength from a determined naturalism in acting and setting, and the central character is played earthily yet reflectively by Patrick Mower. But it is naturalism of a lofty kind, which achieves a variety of visual beauty and effect in harmony with the romantic and poetic quality of the play. Almost the whole of Act Five is presented and, in keeping with the retrospective emphasis of the act, some reminders of earlier parts of the play, particularly those concerned with Aase and Solveig, are included.

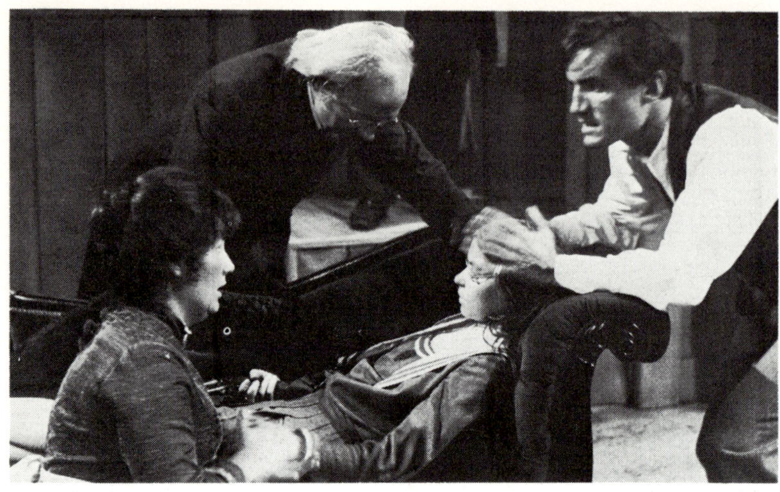

The Wild Duck by Henrik Ibsen
Translated by J. W. McFarlane
A continuous section from the end of Act IV right through Act V, pre-
faced by a short scene from Act I.

Hjalmar Ekdal	Anthony Ainley
Gregers Werle	Michael Bryant
Gina Ekdal	Jo Kendall
Hedvig Ekdal	Veronica Quilligan
Relling	Richard Beale
Old Ekdal	Geoffrey Bayldon
Haakon Werle	John Citroen
Molvik	Tom Durham
Designer	Steve Scott
Director	Nick Levinson

Illustration: *The dead Hedvig (Veronica Quilligan) lamented by her parents (Jo Kendall, l. and Anthony Ainley, r.). Gregers (Michael Bryant) at centre.*

Henrik Ibsen
The Wild Duck (1884)

With *The Wild Duck* we come to perhaps the most densely imagined of the modern plays in this series. The apparent question in the play can be simply stated, but it is not simply treated, and the answer at the end is ambiguous: the question seems to be, 'Is it better to know the whole truth about oneself and one's relationships, or to be content with things as they are, even if contentment includes a degree of self-delusion?' Ibsen had tackled this and related problems previously, most notably in *Brand*, the hero of which is an 'all-or-nothing' man, and *Peer Gynt*, the compromiser who went 'round about' and was judged at the last to be a negative person. Those two plays complement each other. Ibsen wrote *The Wild Duck* after *An Enemy of the People*, a play written with intense verve about a Dr Stockmann who insists on exposing the fact that the water to the town's lucrative spa is tainted, although his action loses him his job and causes his family to be ostracised. So Ibsen seems almost to be laughing at such absolutist heroes as Brand and Stockmann in even entertaining the idea, as he does in *The Wild Duck*, that to bring out the truth might be harmful.

The truths that come out at the end of *The Wild Duck* concern the Ekdal family, Hjalmar and Gina, their fourteen-year-old daughter Hedvig and Old Ekdal, Hjalmar's father. They collect round a doubt about Hedvig. Is she Hjalmar's child, or the child of Haakon Werle whose servant and mistress Gina was until her marriage to Hjalmar? The television programme, in which the climax and end of the play are performed, starts with a short scene between Haakon Werle and his son, Gregers. In it the lines of conflict between father and son, which set in motion the final events, are clearly drawn. For Gregers has come back to his home town to take revenge on his father for having, amongst other things, driven his mother to an unhappy death by having liaisons with other women: and the one thing he can do for certain, he believes, is to make his old friend Hjalmar know exactly how the shadow of Old Werle lies on his little family. Gregers believes it is his mission in life to make people face the truth, and the phrase 'the claims of the ideal', which he uses when as it were preaching his doctrine, occurs repeatedly. As son and father argue, we learn that, long before, Haakon Werle was involved in an illegal tree-felling deal, but escaped the consequences while his associate, Old Ekdal went to prison for it; that Haakon helped his mistress, Gina, perhaps because he feared that she was pregnant, to marry young Hjalmar; and that he compensated the Ekdal family by paying the disgraced Old Ekdal, on his release from prison, to do a copying job in his office, and by helping Hjalmar financially to set up a modest photography business.

The Ekdal family is a strange one. Hjalmar, its head, is a sentimental and self-deluded man, given to self-dramatising; Gina keeps him happy by attending to all his needs and in fact doing most of his professional photography work; and in this she is helped by the growing girl, Hedvig, who is devoted to her parents. Hedvig wears glasses, and her sight is deteriorating rapidly. In the background Old Ekdal shuffles in a senile and often drunken way. Downstairs in another part of the house lives their friend Dr Relling, who puts a sort of common-sense front on life to hide his failures which, so far as we know them, were in his profession and in his love life. He is the ideological opposite of Gregers Werle, because he tries to help people to manage in life by providing them with a 'life-lie': that is to say, an illusion about themselves which helps them to have self-respect and a positive goal.

Ibsen used to compile detailed biographies of his characters before starting to write a play, and only when he had them all clearly in his mind with their special qualities did the play begin to take shape and start to move towards its climax. For three and a half acts, which we do not see in this programme, Ibsen shows the world of these characters in action. After the first short scene between Gregers and his father, we see Gregers and Hjalmar talking. Gregers has been telling Hjalmar what he knows about Haakon, and Hjalmar is trying to adjust to a new view of the events which led up to his marriage. The final action begins when

Hedvig comes in with a deed of gift from Haakon Werle to herself. That, with the knowledge that Hedvig is suffering from the same eye-trouble as Haakon, convinces Hjalmar that Hedvig is not his child, and the tragedy is set in motion.

It would be quite wrong, though understandable, if an audience new to Ibsen were to imagine that his great innovation was a naturalistic manner which allows people to speak in normal tones about everyday life while remaining safely or reluctantly in their ordinary environment. *The Wild Duck* might just conceivably give such an initial impression. But though we may laugh at Hjalmar's naïve soul-searching as he plasters butter on his bread and gulps his coffee, and perhaps even be amused by Old Ekdal's dream-world in the loft, where he keeps animals and birds and actually shoots rabbits, in pale, insane imitation of his former soldiering and hunting glories, our laughter is evoked by much more than recognition of comically discrepant but realistic human traits. *The Wild Duck* is a work so clear in outline, yet so dense and minutely planned, that one needs to listen to the deceptively simple dialogue with all senses alert: to visual and aural suggestion; to the frequent ironic implication; to changes in the time of day and the weather – moonlight, lamplight or bleak snow-glare; to the lighting of lamps and offers of hospitality and comfort in the form of food and drink.

Most of all, we should mark the constant reference to 'the claims of the ideal' because, however facile and intrusive Gregers Werle, the misguided idealist in the play, may be, he nonetheless draws attention to what should be the transforming and redeeming element in human life – an awareness of ultimate truth. As we watch the various members of the Ekdal and Werle families face the demands of daily existence and aspire, in the case of Gregers and Hjalmar, to deeper understanding of what life is about, we find ourselves taken beyond their day-to-day preoccupations and tawdry attempts to philosophise into a hallucinatory but revealing world where the wild duck of the title is both a symbol of freedom and soaring flight and, in its maimed and domesticated state, an appropriate silent comment on the imperfect state of the people engaged in the drama.

In a review written in May 1887 George Bernard Shaw described the effect a performance of *The Wild Duck* had on him:

To look on with horror and pity at a profound tragedy, shaking with laughter all the time at an irresistible comedy: to go out, not from a diversion, but from an experience deeper than real life ever brings to most men, or often brings to any man: that is what *The Wild Duck* was like last Monday ... at the *Globe.*

Shaw's praise emphasises both the profundity of experience conveyed and the tragi-comic mode by which it is achieved. There is a kind of counterpoint running through the play – a theme of tragic suggestion insisting on the deep meaning, and an accompaniment of counter-suggestion (comic, or matter-of-fact, or even witheringly sarcastic, as when Relling is speaking) which distances the spectator from the action while intensifying his understanding and his sympathy with the characters. Shaw was able to respond with both tears and laughter, as it were, to the play's strange duality of impact.

The strange richness of the play is embodied in its title, and to a large extent in the way the bird and the place in which it lives permeate and partly create the meaning of the play, as well as framing the dramatic circumstances. The loft, with its wide space and mystery, is always *there* while action and conversation are going on in the ordinary confined domestic interior in the foreground. It leads off Hjalmar's studio – which also acts as living-room – in the Ekdal's top-floor flat, and is in fact the attic. It is never seen open in the television production, but in theatre performance its entrance is usually big, centrally-placed double doors. They are tugged open dramatically in Act II by the two Ekdal men helped by Hedvig, to show Gregers Werle how Old Ekdal now passes his time, and what, in his drunken senility, has replaced for him 'that open-air life in the forest and on the moors, amongst the beasts and the birds'. Irregularly lit by pools of moonlight, the loft is at the moment an enchanted place with its sleeping hens, rabbits and pigeons, bits of foliage to represent the forest, and sail-cloth and a fishing-net to evoke the sea. Ekdal's dream-world where he spends his days walking, drinking and literally shooting, is the world of nature in miniature, a microcosm.

The main importance of the loft is as the place where Hedvig keeps the wild duck, which came to her after a shooting party in which Haakon Werle wounded it. For the closely knit members of this strange little family, with its self-centred, inadequate men and its devotedly caring women, the wild duck is just a bird, a maimed creature in a basket. But to Gregers, who comes to live in their spare room, the bird becomes a symbol of the Ekdal family's protected life of illusion. Having shattered the peace of the family group, and told Hjalmar of the old affair between his father and Gina, Gregers tries to make Hjalmar transcend these petty realities in response to 'the claim of the ideal'. When Hjalmar thrusts

Gregers persuades Hedvig to sacrifice her wild duck.

Hedvig from him, thinking that she is not his own but Haakon's daughter, Gregers suggests that she kill the wild duck to prove her love for Hjalmar and so win him back as a father. The terrible climax comes when Hedvig shoots herself in the loft; and the family, hearing the shot, imagine at first that Old Ekdal is having one of his routine shoots in there, and then, on the prompting of Gregers, believe that the wild duck has been killed to prove Hedvig's love for Hjalmar.

It is essential that Hedvig – who of all the characters is the one most closely identified with the wild duck – is not glamorised into a nubile and attractive figure of pathos. Veronica Quilligan presents her as a rather ordinary, affectionate girl at the stage of puberty, devoted to her parents and her pet. Hedvig is the only character in the play at whom one never laughs. She achieves final pathos as her dead body

Relling (Richard Beale) comforts Hedvig.

is lifted from the sofa by Hjalmar and Gina, to the accompaniment of Hjalmar's fatuous, self-pitying: 'Oh Gina, can you bear this?' It is part of that beautiful doubleness of the play that Molvik, Relling's drunken friend and an ex-theological student, salutes the corpse with: 'The child is not dead, but sleepeth.' Relling's whispered 'Shut up man! You're drunk!' is one of the many moments when the Doctor tries unsuccessfully to control events. Richard Beale admirably conveys the intelligence and humanity of Relling, as well as the sense of failure and disillusionment with life which, after all, we should expect to find in a man who advances such a defeatist doctrine as that of the 'life-lie'. Michael Bryant is careful not to suggest any evil intention in Gregers, who is structurally the villain of the piece by causing the catastrophe. Rather, he stresses the doubts and self-deludedness of the repressed fanatic, and gives a marvellous *inward* performance. His Gregers means to handle Hedvig with idealistic delicacy, but reveals a faint stirring of sexual interest, which he restrains. It is a sensitive performance which gives the complexity of the character a fine clarity.

Gina, with her down-to-earth sweeping and tidying, and her frequent preparation of food and drink, balances Hjalmar's mercurial melancholy with her matter-of-fact practical sense and concentration on material essentials. She is dominated by her will to hold her family together in love and care. All the same, she too is comic with her inability to find the right words for the philosophical counters bandied by her husband and Gregers. But for true feeling and right thinking, she and Hedvig carry the main sympathy in the play. Gina's limitation is that she is so absorbed by what she regards as her certainties that she does not act in time when they are threatened. But if she had been intelligent and forceful, *The Wild Duck* would have been a different play.

Although the end of the play belongs to Gregers and Relling, in their last debate about values in the shattered air left behind by Hedvig's death, the man we see most of, the character whose inner drama precipitates the tragedy, is Anthony Ainley's Hjalmar. He gives an extraordinary performance, keeping afloat in the air a kind of tragi-comic music. The complexities of the play are marvellously reflected in his wondering, self-absorbed playing of that weak, vain and vulnerable man. What is sad and what is funny are not separated, because we suffer with Hjalmar as we laugh at him. What is real and what is fantasy are not separated either, because what to us appears as his self-deception is to him intense reality. And indeed, to all of us, are not fantasies part of the truth, as that loft and all of which it is a reminder signify?

Three Sisters by Anton Chekhov
Translated by Elisaveta Fen
A section of Act I is followed by the whole of Act III.

Masha	Katharine Schofield
Irena	Tessa Wyatt
Olga	Vivien Heilbron
Vershinin	Jeremy Kemp
Andrey	David Strong
Natasha	Wendy Allnutt
Chebutykin	Mark Dignam
Toozenbach	Ben Kingsley
Koolyghin	George Little
Soliony	Frank Vincent
Fedotik	Mike Savage
Rode	Ian Oliver
Ferrapont	Harold Bennett
Anfisa	Mary Barclay
Designer	Colin Bowles
Director	Nick Levinson

Illustration: *Masha (Katharine Schofield) at lunch between her husband Koolyghin (George Little, r.) and Colonel Vershinin (Jeremy Kemp).*

Anton Chekhov
Three Sisters (1901)

Anton Chekhov (1860–1904) was by profession a doctor. Through long, hard years as a medical student in Moscow, he largely supported his improvident father and poor family by dashing off hundreds of stories and sketches for newspapers and magazines. He began to write prose and poetry as a mere schoolboy living a harsh provincial life, and in later years, as then, he was inclined to refer to his writing, even his most painstakingly constructed plays, as jottings or 'scribblings', something 'dashed off' in the course of a career determined by great effort and integrity. The descriptions are ironical, for he acknowledged the labour that went into his creative work, but such understatement helped him maintain an admirable sense of proportion and perspective.

His first full-length play, *Ivanov*, was produced in Moscow in 1887, when he was twenty-seven. However, soon after that he took a country practice as a doctor and spent more and more time away from Moscow, particularly when failing health in early middle age made necessary the kind of climate he found in the Crimea. It is unusual to discover a playwright of his time, when travel was still difficult and exhausting, living so far from the theatres, directors and actors essential to his art. But his happy marriage, latish in life – though he died when only forty-four – to the actress Olga Knipper, who played leading roles in *The Seagull, Uncle Vanya, Three Sisters* and *The Cherry Orchard* and went on playing them for forty years after his death, gave him a vital link with the theatre in which they were staged.

This was the Moscow Art Theatre. In 1898, looking for a play that would provide a natural rather than rhetorical and 'stagy' production, its director, Stanislavsky, the theatrical innovator and theorist whose writings, particularly on acting, have been of major influence in this century, persuaded Chekhov to let him put on *The Seagull*. In spite of the dramatist's misgivings and its failure when first produced in 1896, it was a brilliant success: it was also the beginning of a working alliance between the two men which, although not always one of agreement and shared vision, lasted until Chekhov's death in 1904. As Stanislavsky is primarily associated with the change to a naturalistic approach in Russian theatre, it is not surprising that we find references to Chekhov also as a 'father of naturalist drama'. Yet there is nothing crude or blatantly lifelike in Chekhov's art, which is an infinitely delicate affair of fining things down to a few revelatory details, which gradually expose a personality or mode of life. The detail in itself is true to nature, but it also evokes impressions and truths far beyond the scope of photographic representation.

Chekhov's dialogue has a special quality of suggestion; it is rarely a dramatic instrument of confrontation and exchange, like Ibsen's. There are some direct interchanges between the characters, but often what they say is in the form of subtle monologues, which sometimes interweave and then glance apart again. The characters are mostly isolated, and their words seem to fall on their own ears alone. In the theatre, the actor's response to Chekhov's technique must be to play with a sense of the character's individuality, and to relate naturally and intimately with other characters in a new kind of group performance which does not always depend on logical sequence of speech and action: 'unselfish' acting is essential. In this television programme, the individual and group playing are harmonised by sensitive camera direction which, by alternating close-ups and wide shots, finds the rhythms and complexities of the play. Director and actors combine to produce a near-perfect Chekhovian image.

In *Three Sisters*, there is a pattern of interrelated soliloquies in which several characters reveal their inner selves. Such is the effect produced by Vershinin, the newly arrived Lieutenant-Colonel, speaking in the first act of his unhappy marriage and much-loved children; by Koolyghin bouncing in with schoolmasterly self-importance to gloat over an invitation to his director's house for a country walk; by Andrey in the dead hours of the night after the fire thinking that he is listened to by two of his sisters as he explains his professional failure, his commonplace marriage and the heavy debts which have forced him to mortgage the family home. Perhaps most poignant of all in this production is the short focus on the old doctor as he laments his lack of skill, memory and knowledge while sluicing his face and hands with water as if he had just performed an operation or helped combat the fire.

The great exception to this self-preoccupied isolation is found in the three sisters, Olga, Masha and Irena, who can retire from the wounding everyday world to confide in each other. Masha is married to the bumptious, thick-skinned teacher Koolyghin, Olga is a frustrated schoolmistress herself, and Irena, the youngest, as yet uncommitted, is in love with the idea of work. They are united by memories of their dead parents, of the happy life they led as children in Moscow, by their longing to return there, and by their struggle against tedious provincial existence.

The final part of the first Act, which forms the opening scene in the television production, shows the family and their friends celebrating the twentieth anniversary of Irena's saint's day. As Chekhov prescribed in his stage directions, Olga wears 'the regulation dark-blue dress of a secondary school mistress', Masha is 'in black' and Irena 'in white'. They are strongly differentiated in type but the two elder girls share a strained look and pallor. They move among their guests; and the delicate suggestion of formal groupings as they converse before the anniversary meal contrasts strongly with the jolly, almost free-for-all atmosphere at the table itself. There the old Nanny sits at one end mopping up her soup with black bread, Masha strikes her knife upon her glass in request for red wine, and the ageing doctor, Chebutykin, makes his comically outrageous comments. Arriving late for luncheon with a basket of flowers for Irena, two young officers are welcomed noisily. One of them has a camera and, when Irena and her guests 'freeze' to be photographed, the sudden halt to activity and the conscious happy posing for posterity make a golden moment.

The conversation before lunch has already suggested certain pairings. Masha is, of course, married to Koolyghin but it becomes rapidly obvious that they do not form a real couple: she is made of much finer clay than her insensitive, but in his own way loving, husband. Irena is courted by the baron, Toozenbach, who seems an odd little man despite his title and his uniform; he in fact wants to leave the army, and shares with Irena a vision of working hard in order to make life purposeful. The third pair consists of Andrey, the girls' brother, and Natasha, whose concern for her own appearance and lack of taste in dress suggest a superficial and vain temperament. She cannot bear to feel inferior or under

Olga (Vivien Heilbron) criticises the belt of Natasha (Wendy Allnutt).

attack and, sensing hostility in the broad banter and teasing at the table, she rushes away. But the adoring Andrey, who is determined to marry her, consoles her. In this introductory scene we see these couples as they come together and are caught by the camera, then the focus changes to the larger group.

The significant grouping is carried through into the night-scene in Act III, which is presented in full in the television programme. The setting is an upstairs bedroom in the family home that the sisters now share with Andrey, Natasha and their young children. The room is in darkness except for occasional pools of light cast by table lamps and although it is two o'clock in the morning, there is continual coming and going, for a fire rages in the town and normal life is disrupted. Olga and Irena usually sleep here but now, while Masha rests wearily on a settee, they busy themselves with problems caused by the fire. Vivien Heilbron, Katharine Schofield and Tessa Wyatt as the three sisters, directed with kindly visual imagination, suggest a family closeness with their uniformly fair hair and assured, quiet playing to each other. Their blondeness above pale, strained faces catches the lamplight. As other people enter the shadowy, intimate room they are momentarily illuminated in

Irena (Tessa Wyatt) and Toozenbach (Ben Kingsley) sitting up on the night of the fire. In the background (l. to r.) Vershinin, Chebutykin (Mark Dignam) and Koolyghin.

the open doorway, then gravitate towards the lamplit oases in the warm gloom. The whole scene is beautifully constructed like a choreographed dance – in which the characters may have solo parts, or join one with another in a *pas de deux*, or combine to form a chorus. Singly or in groups they come in turn under the gentle spotlights of the opaque white lamps, and each 'movement' or grouping thus has its own focal point of light. By this device the single speaker is isolated not only as constantly happens in Chekhov, in his own thoughts, but also physically in an island of dim light; by contrast, a couple or group forming a tableau on the settee or round a small table produce an immediate visual image of their attempt to comfort or communicate.

The viewer becomes poignantly aware of the developing pattern of lonely monologue set against dialogue or social conversation when Chebutykin, played seriously with moving restraint by Mark Dignam, comes in alone after drinking and goes to the washstand by the far wall. Soaping his hands and rubbing them together with a suggestion of washing dirt out of his life, he stands there by himself, despairing at his inadequacy as doctor and as man. His quietly-spoken words seem to express a modern existential anguish: 'Perhaps I don't exist at all, and I only imagine that I'm walking and eating and sleeping ... Oh! if only I could stop existing.' His tortured soliloquy is punctuated by glimpses of the grinning, uncomprehending face of Koolyghin who has foolishly hidden in the wardrobe to see what the doctor would get up to.

This monologue, according to the alternating scheme, gives way to a group conversation with the doctor seated between the Battery Commander, Vershinin, and Baron Toozenbach, who have just arrived from the burning town and are concerned about the catastrophe. There is talk of the local military leaving for Poland or Siberia. This upsets the girls and Irena takes refuge in the idea that the sisters repeatedly comfort themselves with in time of stress: 'We'll go away, too'. Chebutykin drops the china clock he has been examining silently, and like the precious ornament the group is splintered and the tableau dissolves.

It is now Vershinin's turn to move forward into the spotlight, and to muse – as if the others were asleep – on the events of the night and his fears for his children's safety. He is exhilarated by activity, and 'philosophises' (his own word) about the way in which human life will surely now improve. Nothing could contrast more with the doctor's despair. Masha, who had left the room, enters unobserved and sits listening, growing radiant in response to this expression of hope, and perhaps to his previously-declared love for her. He gradually becomes aware of her presence and the monologue expands into dialogue as she matches his elation by singing raptly and quietly, in reply to him; both of them lost momentarily in wonder and love for one another. Katharine Schofield as Masha gives a beautifully shaded performance; and here we see the coiled spring of her nervous frustration relax gently before the endearing optimism of Jeremy Kemp's Vershinin. Then the couple are interrupted by the arrival of another victim of the fire, and the 'chorus' of characters reappears from the surrounding shadows and assembles about the newcomer.

The love of Masha and Vershinin is, of course, metaphorically encompassed in gloom like the room in which it is tacitly declared, for each is married to another. But fundamentally Masha lacks the destructive energy of an Anna Karenina or a Madame Bovary, and is enervated by the weariness and inactivity of provincial life. In fact, when the family is eventually alone, and her husband shows unwelcome concern for her and a contentment with his own lot, both of which are ironically timed, she explodes with the words, 'And I'm so bored, bored, bored!'

Having persuaded Koolyghin to go home, the three sisters are at last together undisturbed. Each reveals the turbulence which had been hidden behind the social mask. Irena echoes the sense of irreparable loss we heard earlier in the doctor's outpourings: 'Where has it all gone to? Where is it? Oh, God! I've forgotten ... I've forgotten everything ... life's slipping by, and it will never, never come back ... We shall never go to Moscow ... I can see that we shall never go ...' In comforting her and advising her to marry the Baron, Olga discloses her own utter loneliness and feeling of rejection: 'I'd marry anyone who proposed to me, as long as he was a decent man. I'd even marry an old man!' This soul-baring declaration prompts Masha to confess to Olga and Irena her hopeless love for Vershinin. Olga scolds and refuses the inadmissible idea, but Irena comes to her seated on the couch and puts her arms about her, so that the two gleaming heads draw together in sympathy and longing. Such moments, softly illuminated against the outer darkness, throw into relief the unavailing efforts of those who try to make contact, to connect with others, and fail. Andrey, who is the last to impede the sisters' attempts to get to bed, is so keen to explain his professional failure and his debts to them, and to defend Natasha his wife, that he does not even realise they have vanished from sight. His anguished cry of eventual recognition, 'So you won't listen ...', points to that difficulty of establishing contact which the visual imagery and the overall visual concept of the scene were designed to illustrate.

Here the programme ends, and Act IV, the final scene of departures and farewell, can be regarded as a coda to the delicate defining of relationship and individual predicaments which has unfolded before us. The end of the play confirms the worst fears regarding the hopes and plans of these vulnerable creatures of Chekhov's, who are more acted upon than acting. The regiment prepares to leave; Olga has become a headmistress – but not a wife; Masha must say goodbye to Vershinin, sobbing openly in front of her husband, who is not unsympathetic but radiates more self-confidence than ever after his recent promotion; Irena has a temporary vision of possible reprieve from unhappiness by marriage to Toozenbach, but at the very end Chebutykin brings news that Soliony, who has earlier appeared ominously as a rather irrational enemy of the Baron, has killed him in a duel. The commonplace and second-rate survive best: Koolyghin rattles away happily about school, and the triumphant Natasha crudely plans for the time when she will be sole mistress of the house, as both Olga and Irena will live and work away from home. Only the old doctor is unmoved, for he is beyond hope, beyond despair. 'What does it matter?' he asks; 'Nothing matters!' – to which Olga replies 'If only we knew, if only we knew!'

The Ghost Sonata by August Strindberg
Translated by Michael Meyer
The last two of three 'movements' with some flashbacks to the first.

Hummel	Joseph O'Conor
The Mummy	Beatrix Lehmann
The Student	David Troughton
The Daughter	Anne Kidd
The Colonel	Frank Middlemass
Bengtsson	Gerald Cross
Johansson	Paddy Joyce
The Cook	Hope Jackman
The Milkmaid	Susie Blake
Designer	Colin Bowles
Director	Richard Callanan

Illustration: *The Daughter (Anne Kidd) dying in the Hyacinth Room.*

August Strindberg
The Ghost Sonata (1907)

To see Strindberg's *The Ghost Sonata* after Chekhov's *Three Sisters* is like moving from a world of finely perceived actuality peopled by rounded characters to one of fantasy, in which the characters are possessed by nightmare motives and obsessions, and are continually erupting in violence of feeling and action. But fantasy, as we saw in *The Wild Duck*, is an essential part of reality, whether.it is presented naturalistically or expressionistically. Strindberg's reputation as an original dramatic genius who has profoundly influenced modern theatre is based on both his innovations as a playwright and his insight into the human condition. If the latter seems to be mainly concerned with extreme and even pathological states of being, we should remember that in psychology it is often the strangest facets that teach us most about what specialists above all refrain from calling 'normality'.

August Strindberg (1849–1912) wrote about fifty plays, covering a huge range of subjects in many different ways. He wrote dramas of Swedish history, poetic and symbolic plays, some of them mystical and religious, and a number of so-called naturalistic plays, such as *The Father*, *Miss Julie* and *The Dance of Death*, on which his chief fame in Britain rests. *The Ghost Sonata* belongs to the last phase of Strindberg's career as a dramatist. In 1907 he went into partnership with the young actor and director August Falck, whose ambition was to give Strindberg's plays the productions they deserved. Together they set up the Intimate Theatre in Stockholm, and Strindberg, in a ten-week burst of creativity, wrote three expressionist 'chamber plays', as he called them, the last of which was *The Ghost Sonata*. His achievement in these and other plays brought him fame on the continent as the great exponent of expressionist drama, but not in Britain, which has never accommodated to the mode. In Germany alone, in the three years 1913–15, there were 1035 performances of twenty-four different plays by Strindberg.

But *The Ghost Sonata* should not be approached simply through a notion about Strindberg as a dramatic dealer in the intense and the abnormal. Behind his achievement in this last group of plays lay a lifetime of play-writing and fundamental thinking about drama and the theatre; modern reforms and subsequent developments cannot be seriously discussed without reference to his ideas about the writing and staging of plays. He was deeply critical of the consistency of dramatic character that he found in plays of most periods, even those by major dramatists such as Molière; only Shakespeare satisfied him, by creating real characters such as we meet in life, complex and often inconsistent. In his preface to *Miss Julie* (1888) Strindberg describes his own characters as 'agglomerations of past and present cultures, scraps from books and newspapers, fragments of humanity, torn shreds of once-fine clothing that has become rags, in just the way that a human soul is patched together' (Michael Meyer's translation). And in dialogue, he worked against logically sequential talk among characters, but in a different way from Chekhov: he 'allowed their minds to work irregularly, as people's do in real life'. From actors he demanded unobtrusive, naturalistic performance, with an intelligent awareness both of character, and relationships among characters. In his letters to the Intimate Theatre company, he was particularly biting about the kind of star actor who tried to act other actors off the stage, and did not even read the script except for his own part, so that he could not contribute to a harmonious interpretation of the whole play.

Strindberg also had many ideas about staging which, taken together, amount to a way of both intensifying and simplifying the image and impact of a play. For instance, he decried heavy artificial make-up and the distorting effect of footlights, and wanted strong natural light from the wings and from above on minimally made-up faces. He also decried both artificial scenery, with 'waving' doors and walls made of canvas, and cluttered 'realistic' sets intended to look like fully-furnished rooms. He wanted solid practical sets, and furniture and properties strictly limited to what was essential in the play. He wished his plays to be presented without intervals, so that the audience might receive the full impact of their meaning and rhythm without distraction amid the banalities of bar and foyer. Lastly, the word 'intimate' in the name of his theatre evokes the kind of dramatic experience Strindberg strove to give: something close, shared and intense, as far as possible from that provided in the huge old traditional theatres, where star performers, framed by artificial perspective scenery and sustained by ponderous stage machinery, bellowed their agonies and joys to a distant gallery.

In calling his play *The Ghost Sonata*, Strindberg wanted to draw attention to what he believed was its quasi-musical structure. He thought of a play as working not by the mechanics of action and character, but by the statement, development and resolution of themes, like a sonata. So the play has three 'movements' – like a sonata – each with its own thematic arrangement and characteristics, each related to the other movements. He had in mind Beethoven's Pianoforte Sonata in D minor, Op. 31 no. 2, which affected him so strongly that he called it 'the ghost sonata'; and he wanted bars 96–107 of the last movement played during the performance of the play, to signify its musical motif. It is rapid, turbulent music.

Strindberg considered Beethoven the greatest of all artists, and kept a bust of him in his study. He also had there a statue of the Buddha. His religion was distinctly eclectic, based on Christianity but permeated with oriental beliefs such as those of Buddhism, which are especially important in *The Ghost Sonata*. Buddhism teaches that suffering, which is caused by desire, can end only with the suppression of desire through discipline and, ultimately, with the achievement of *nirvana*, which is the extinction of passion and individual existence through absorption into the supreme spirit.

The third ever-present emblem in Strindberg's study was a stuffed owl, which he regarded as his talisman for wishing evil and curses on his imagined persecutors. Strindberg seemed incapable of sustaining harmonious relationships, and usually turned most savagely on those to whom he had been closest. *The Ghost Sonata* was written towards the end of his life, when he was becoming increasingly neurotic and pessimistic, and when terminal cancer of the stomach may have been taking a grip on him. Its main themes are the power of evil, guilt and expiation, and despair.

The Ghost Sonata offers a black vision: life is horrifying and mostly pretence, and people live mainly by destroying others. The broad lines of action in this dramatic nightmare – which like most nightmares contains absurdities as well as terrors – are not complicated, and in the programme the second and third movements are presented complete, with four flashbacks to significant moments in the first movement which reinforce the themes. In the first movement, outside a big house Hummel, an old cripple, meets a student whom he wants to marry his daughter. She is the child of his former lover, who lives in the house with her husband, a Colonel whom Hummel wishes to destroy. The second and third scenes take place inside the house. The second, the 'ghost supper' scene, begins with the servants of the Colonel and Hummel talking about their masters and others: then Hummel comes in uninvited, to expose the falsity of the Colonel and, he hopes, to evict him and his family and establish the Student with his Daughter in the house. But the Colonel's wife intervenes to expose Hummel in turn for his past cruelty and crimes; and, having lost his hold on them, Hummel dies. In the third scene, in the Hyacinth Room, the Student and Daughter seem to go through the main stages of a relationship, from courtship, through a humdrum marriage, to final separation through death.

The programme opens with Bengtsson, the Colonel's footman, showing Johansson, Hummel's servant, the strange drawing-room. They dis-

Johansson (Paddy Joyce) and Bengtsson (Gerald Cross) inspect the Mummy (Beatrix Lehmann) in her cupboard.

cuss their superiors, and the objects in the room which come to have symbolic meaning, in comic, almost disbelieving terms as the camera moves round. The Colonel's wife, who spends most of her time in a cupboard as a parrot, is made briefly to perform. We see the oriental screen which they put out 'when someone's going to die'; the long-case clock, 'the clock of death on the wall', the time of which can be accelerated or stopped; the statue of the Colonel's wife, 'the Mummy', when young; and a long shot shows us the Hyacinth Room, where the pale Daughter sits near the Buddha and a harp, surrounded by hyacinths. Like the ghost of the Milkmaid drowned by Hummel, whom we see only in flashback, she is one of the wasting anaemic girls of the kind that always fascinated Strindberg – the very opposite of the three active professional women whom he married and separated from during his lifetime. The Milkmaid, being dead, is no longer susceptible to life's corruption, and when she appears it is as Hummel's accusing judge, the sight of whom he cannot bear on account of his guilt. But the Daughter will live through her life of corruption in swift time in the third movement.

The two conversing servants are interrupted by Hummel, who steals on them unawares on crutches, vampire-like, and sends them away. Joseph O'Conor as Hummel establishes at once an image of a satanic creature imprisoned in some terrible scheme of things. As he looks round the room – pausing to adjust his wig as the Colonel does later (wig is *pretence*) – the Mummy enters, and they discuss their guilt over their past love (which is the Mummy's reason for living in the cupboard in shame) and Hummel's intention to punish the Colonel for having seduced his fiancée long before. The Mummy warns Hummel to spare the Colonel, and when they hear the latter coming, she goes back into her cupboard. The Colonel comes in, and Hummel quickly strips him of all his pretences – his possessions first, then his nobility, and lastly his military rank. It is one of several symbolic strippings in which the pretences are mercilessly ripped off and characters are left to wither or die. (Bergmann in one of his productions of *The Ghost Sonata* did leave the Colonel physically naked.)

The Student now appears and the Colonel, whom Hummel had revealed as a former footman, resumes his pretences and moral superiority. The guests, a 'Baron Skanskorg', apparently a jewel thief, and Hummel's former fiancée, Mademoiselle Beata von Holsteinkrona, totter in, and the party of corrupted old folk are complete for the 'ghost supper'. As Hummel condemns them all and prepares for his own triumph – in the narration of which he boasts of having 'once summoned a drowning girl back to life' – the Milkmaid appears and terrifies him. Then, as Hummel waits for the clock to strike the hour of his victory, the Mummy stops the clock, and begins her stripping of Hummel with the advice that they can only 'wipe out the past ... with suffering and contrition'. With the help of Bengtsson, she reveals all his cruel and criminal past, including the fact that he had begun life as a servant. He exposes even his latest 'benefaction', his intention of marrying the Student to his Daughter, as the theft of the Student's soul. We have already seen that Hummel's vampire hold on the Student is a literal one: when they shake hands, the Student goes icy cold and feels that his strength is being drained away.

All Hummel's power goes with his exposure. As he paddles into the cupboard to his death and the old people say 'Amen!', the camera takes us slowly into the Hyacinth Room, which the Daughter calls 'the place of trial'. From here onward, David Troughton as the Student and Ann Kidd as the Daughter ably sustain the long, declining mood and time shifts till the play ends. We hear harp music, which the Daughter plays as the Student sings a song in praise of life and innocence. But even as together they contemplate the possibility of achieving heaven on earth, the suffocating influence of Hummel and of the corruption of life oozes into their dream. The hyacinths, with their promise of heaven, stifle the Student with their scent and the Daughter, oppressed by the life of the old people, quotes a remark of the Colonel's which must surely be the ultimate cynicism about relationship: 'What is the point of talking? We cannot deceive each other.'

A new character, the Cook ('How big and fat she is ... one of the Hummels – that breed of vampires!') comes in to sap their remaining strength further. The Daughter is in her power, just as Hummel and the Colonel were helplessly bound to, and dependent on, their servants. The Cook brings with her not just dread, but a foetid sense of the disorder, dirt and slime of domestic life – another of Strindberg's real-life obsessions. The Student tries to make the Daughter sing, and so resist the creeping death, but he is unsuccessful, and we are reminded, in a flashback to the first movement, of his hopeless longing for her when she passed him and Hummel in the square outside the house. He had wept because 'when one gazes at the unattainable, what else can one do but despair?'

Quite suddenly it seems, the Student, Hamlet-like, asks the Daughter, 'Do you love honesty?' and what spills from him is an 'honest' descrip-

The Student (David Troughton) tries to arouse the dying Daughter.

tion of all the terrible evil he has seen around him. He ends the catalogue by doubting whether the Daughter alone could be pure in such a world, and begs her to sing to him in order to prove her honour and faith in him. Weakening towards death, she cannot, and when he tries to play the harp himself, the strings make no music. Bengtsson brings in the screen and the Daughter, who has been ageing throughout her trials, dies, while the Student prays to Christ and Buddha for purity of will, and sings again the song in praise of life and innocence.

In this production the Student sings that song as a dying man, but then the Mummy brings in Hummel's crutches on which he goes out into life – or perhaps into the cupboard? The impression is given that the Mummy has expiated her guilt, and that the Student may expiate his, in a way that Hummel never could. It is an interpretation that attempts to reconcile the conflict in the play between human despair and religious hope; but however the plays ends, the final focus must be on Strindberg's fundamental idea: beatific paradise exists, but since it cannot be reached, man's recourse is despair. But the melancholy music, the Student's prayer for the Daughter's soul, and the fading of the room into Böcklin's romantic picture, *The Island of the Dead*, of which Strindberg kept a copy on the Intimate Theatre's proscenium arch, give the play a coda of gently glooming acceptance.

Six Characters in Search of an Author by Luigi Pirandello
Translated by Frederick May
The middle section of the play (Act II) with a condensed version of the opening.

The Characters

The Father	Nigel Stock
The Mother	Mary Wimbush
The Stepdaughter	Lisa Harrow
The Son	Anthony Chambers
The Boy	Ashley Knight
The Child	Jane Muldoon
Madame Pace	Claire Davenport

The Actors and Company

The Producer	Charles Gray
Leading Lady	Diana Fairfax
Leading Man	John Westbrook
Second Actress	Richenda Carey
Third Actress	Jennifer Guy
Juvenile Lead	Michael Cochrane
Designer	Dacre Punt
Director	John Selwyn Gilbert

Illustration: *The Actors at rehearsal ponder the Characters.*

Luigi Pirandello
Six Characters in Search of an Author (1921)

This play, with its theatrical discoveries, is central to the development of modern drama. In it Pirandello goes beyond Strindberg in questioning the absolute reality of character; Strindberg found it in a state of flux, and looked for a solution, some possible relief from the burden of knowing who he was, in religion. Luigi Pirandello (1867–1936) found circumstances so overwhelmingly dominant that in 1933 he wrote, 'There is someone who is living my life. And I know nothing about him.' That is about as far as it is possible to go from the characters in Ibsen's or Chekhov's plays, whose qualities, however complex and subtly portrayed, make up complete and understandable human beings. The reality of Shaw's and Brecht's characters, and to a lesser extent Ibsen's, is enhanced by a positive sense of the society they live in, and of what that society might become, as an environment in which people wither or flourish. In Chekhov's plays, too, an apparently unalterable but actually changing real society pulses away in the very air the characters breathe. But neither the hope of religion nor a positive view of a concrete world and its human organisations is found in Pirandello, whose characters are rooted in no soil except their own intensity of experience, the existence of which alone gives them the urge to survive, even if it does not give them a formulable aim in life. In this respect Pirandello stands behind Sartre and Camus and Genet, and his characters are as isolated, as variously defiant of the inexplicability of life's continuum, and as funny and as sad, as Beckett's.

Six Characters in Search of an Author begins in a way which was revolutionary fifty years ago, and has been copied many times by theatre directors since. 'When the audience enters the auditorium the curtain is up and the stage is just as it would be during the daytime. There is no set and there are no wings; it is empty and in almost total darkness.' Slowly the routine processes of rehearsal begin; the Stage Manager clears away a hammering Foreman, and the Actors and Actresses dribble in gossiping; the Producer obtains order, and starts to rehearse Pirandello's *The Game As He Played It.*

The rehearsal has hardly begun when Six Characters press into the theatre and through their spokesman, the Father, explain that they are characters who have been abandoned by their author without being used, and that they must play their 'terrible and grievous drama'. The Producer eventually agrees to use their drama as the basis of a play, and the rest of *Six Characters in Search of an Author* consists of scenes from their life presented in interaction with the characters who are 'real' in the world of the play as the audience first apprehend it – that is, the members of the theatre company assembled for rehearsal.

But it turns out that the 'fixed reality' lies in the Characters, who are creations of art eternally bound to the relationships and emotions inherent in the events which they must ceaselessly relive. The shadowy 'real' people with their shallow everyday concerns are dwarfed by the power and passions of these Characters. But more than that: the theatre itself, with its trivial notions of what is good drama, and its limiting conventions concerning what can and what cannot be staged, is made to seem a tawdry place when invaded by the majesty and intensity of the fixed tragedy of the Characters. So two ideas advance together as the drama unfolds: ordinary 'reality' is unreal in both form and substance, and art is the higher and only reality. The Characters themselves are described as 'created realities'.

The peculiar intensity of the play lies in the extra dimensions given to the life of the Characters by the Pirandellian device of 'teatro nel teatro' (theatre within a theatre). It is not only that they are forced to relive their eternal present before others, whose reaction and interaction become part of our own theatre experience; but also that, as their tragedy jerkily unfolds, in anything but chronological order, the Characters argue in pain over what is happening. Like people in real life, they often disagree not only about their motivation, but also in their versions of crucial events. So, although through this process we know more about them and can thus identify with them more closely, we are also, like them, uncertain about the precise nature of the intensely felt reality that they represent. And the suspense works with double force because the performance of the climaxes, of which there are two, are long delayed.

The 'story' the Characters embody is as follows. A man, the Father, marries a simple woman, the Mother, and they have a child, the Son. The Father notices that his secretary is in love with the Mother, and sends them away together. The infant Son, left behind, is boarded out with a peasant woman until old enough to live with the Father. He grows up a loveless, repressed child who will never forgive his Mother for deserting him. Mother and secretary have three children, the Stepdaughter, the Boy and the Little Girl. The Father watches the new family from a distance until the secretary takes them out of the district. When the secretary dies, the Mother of the now-destitute family takes in sewing for a Madame Pace, whose dress-shop is a 'front' for a brothel. Madame Pace lures the Stepdaughter into prostitution; when the Father, not knowing who she is, visits her as a client, the Mother arrives, and the first crisis, which is the core of the television programme, takes place.

Madame Pace (Claire Davenport) instructs the Step-Daughter (Lisa Harrow) in her duties as a prostitute.

The second, at the end of the play, develops when the Father, having thus found his wife and her children, takes them home to make a new start. But the tensions and guilts of the two branches of the family result in the deaths of the two small children and the flight of the Stepdaughter, who ends the play by rushing out through the auditorium, laughing hideously.

Small wonder that at the end of the first performance, in Rome, pandemonium broke out: people shook their fists at Pirandello and shouted 'Clown! Clown!', and their violence had to be restrained by the police. Their sense of expectation in the theatre had been outraged and, on top of that, they had been shaken by the intense enactment of a tragedy which turned on such unsavoury matters as incest and prostitution. In Britain the following year, the Lord Chamberlain forbade the play's public presentation because he thought it 'too disturbing', and only the initiative of Shaw secured a private performance by the Stage Society. Although, in the half-century since *Six Characters* was first seen, its theatre technique has become commonplace and its subject-matter acceptable, its dramatic force and vision of life continue to disturb: it always succeeds in the theatre.

In preparing *Six Characters* for television, the director must decide how to render the theatre setting of the play in television-studio terms. As in the theatre, the beginning of the play, in which the convention is set up and made to work in a way that the viewer can follow, is crucial. For this programme, with its fifty-minute limit, the opening had to be short and make maximum impact, in preparation for the scene of crisis in Madame Pace's dress-shop. So Studio A at Alexandra Palace was set up as a studio for rehearsal – and that meant just as careful work as preparing a theatre stage without a set of any kind, because the action needs this specific setting. The actors are anglicised, and at the start two are playing Chopsticks on a tinny piano as the Leading Man comes in, sits down and starts doing *The Times* crossword. The Producer comes in from the eastern exit; so does the Leading Lady a moment or two later, with her extravagantly ample pug in her arms. All are dressed in late 1940s' style; since the subject-matter, and the way it is handled by the Actors, belong to an age of censorship, it seemed essential to avoid a 1970s' setting. The Leading Man begins to work and as with fatuous self-admiration he 'turns to camera a bit more' as directed, his gaze becomes alarmedly incredulous; for the huge sliding door of the studio has rumbled open and there, motionless in line abreast in the corridor, are the Six Characters.

The Producer (Charles Gray, centre) with members of his puzzled company.

Pirandello's instructions to producers about the Six Characters stress how important it is to avoid any confusion between them and the Actors. He mentions grouping, lighting and, above all, flexible half-masks to give them their main characteristics, 'Remorse for the Father, Revenge for the Stepdaughter, Contempt for the Son and Sorrow for the Mother'. And he wants them not to 'appear as phantoms, but as ... unchangeable creations of the imagination and, therefore, more real and more consistent than the ever-changing naturalness of the Actors'.

The studio means of emphasising the differences between the two groups, and of giving the Characters their separate kind of essentiality, are in some respects stronger and in others weaker than those available in the theatre. For example, on the stage the performers can be grouped separately in a way that is continuously apparent to the audience, but on television, where the camera selects what is seen all the time, grouping must be suggested in some other way. So the director establishes a gently lit part of the studio as a kind of working base for the Actors and another part, a highly lit area with a white floor, as a talking and 'performing' place for the Characters, which is also used by the Actors when rehearsing. Then, the Actors appear mostly in long shot, so that even when there is a close-up of an Actor or Actress, the visual memory is of the group background. But when the Leading Man and Leading Lady move into the Characters' space to rehearse their version of the meeting between Father and Stepdaughter in Madame Pace's shop, they are not distanced in that way.

The main means of giving particularity to the Characters is in a comprehensive presentation style involving acting, gesture, costume and make-up. The Actors are made up naturalistically, but the Characters all have a waxen pallor, with certain features, such as the Stepdaughter's lips, starkly realised. Stage practice has usually rejected the masks Pirandello suggested; as on television, a formal equivalent, mask-like make-up, is generally used. Then, while the Actors flaunt informal gaiety in clothing style and colour, the Characters are formally dressed in dark clothes of the 1920s.

But those differences are, though necessary, superficial, useful initially for establishing the Characters as a separate set of people. The real means of making the Characters what they are is the dramatic realisation of a powerful text by deeply interiorised acting. The Characters, after all, always speak from the depths of their suffering souls; they have no small talk, and no concerns but the terrible passions which move them. Being therefore always at the top of their bent, they present the performers with the problem of generating continuous intensity and fixity without any suggestion of melodrama. And the eye of the camera is much closer to the face of an actor than the eyes of a theatre audience, so that any falsity or crudity of expression is caught at once.

Nigel Stock as the Father and Lisa Harrow as the Stepdaughter play their battle against each other, using the Producer as a sounding-board, with a controlled intensity which seems to exclude all artifice, but is of course the product of disciplined imagination and emotion. Even their still faces blast out the suffering of the Characters. The Father's deeply troubled self-justification and painful theorising, and the Stepdaughter's self-disgust and exhibitionism as she deliberately hurts the Father or scorns the contempt of the Son, are there in the camera's eye, lacerating us. Against these two is poised Charles Gray's Producer, eloquent, graceful in gesticulation, intelligent but essentially trivial, as he tries to cope with a situation which is never in his control, and with a tragedy too big to fit into his trinket-box of a commercial theatre. So that, even as we are lacerated, we are often made to laugh. The small parts have the same intensity as the big ones. Mary Wimbush as the Mother, with her one long explanation of herself and her sorrow, and her appalled

The Step-Daughter and the Father (Nigel Stock) relive the seduction.

interruption of the seduction scene, achieves rare pathos, and Claire Davenport as Madame Pace, red-wigged and enormous, chills with her supernatural arrival and menaces comically with her professional domination of the Stepdaughter.

Six Characters in Search of an Author is a grotesque play, a tragic farce. Pirandello expresses in it all the pessimism probably derived in part from his experience in looking after a deranged wife for twenty years. His force and his bitter humour, his intellectual and psychological approach to the problems of being, are in tune with our age, and his dramatic technique remains a wonder. And this is not true of his theatrical devices only. The long speeches, whether of the Characters or the Producer, are like arias, rhythmic and varied, overwhelmingly dramatic in the impact they make and their furtherance of the themes and action of the play.

The Exception and the Rule by Bertolt Brecht
Translated by Tom Osborn
Performed in full with the music written by Frank Wagland for the
first British performance in 1956.

The Merchant	Patrick Troughton
The Judge	Denholm Elliott
The Coolie	Ben Kingsley
The Guide	Malcolm Terris
The Landlord	Peter Bland
The Coolie's Wife	Souad Faress
Policemen/Assessors	Roy Marsden
	Bunny Reed
The Pianist	Dee Griffiths
Designer	David Hitchcock
Director	Richard Callanan

Illustration: *The two witnesses, the Landlord (Peter Bland) and the Guide
(Malcolm Terris), and the Coolie's Wife (Souad Faress), at the trial of the
Merchant (Patrick Troughton).*

Bertolt Brecht
The Exception and the Rule (1930)

The strongest single influence on theatre practice in the last fifty years
has been that of Bertolt Brecht (1898–1956). His plays, dramatic theory,
stage-directing and training of actors represent a coherent pattern of
ideas about the purpose and function of the theatre which excited,
enthused or antagonised his contemporaries, but in any case could not
be ignored. He died in 1956 only days before he was due to come to
England for the first time with his world-famous theatre company, the
Berliner Ensemble. The group had been founded by Brecht and his wife,
Helene Weigel, in a state-subsidised theatre on the waterfront in East
Berlin at the invitation of the East German government shortly after the
Second World War. As a man of Marxist sympathies, active within
the German Communist Party, Brecht had had to leave Germany on
the rise of fascism in the 1930s. For fifteen years he and his family were
virtual exiles, shifting from one European country to another, and they
finally found a measure of security, but not prosperity, in the United
States. His return in 1947 to East Germany was not only a homecoming
but the realisation of a theatrical and ideological purpose. The Theater
am Schiffbauerdamm, in the heart of the working-class area where he
was to spend the rest of his life (although he took Austrian nationality
in 1950) gave Brecht the opportunity to produce the plays he had written
in exile (*Mother Courage and her Children*, *The Caucasian Chalk Circle*,
The Life of Galileo, *The Good Woman of Setzuan*), and in so doing, to
put into practice his ideas about life and its relation to drama, which

he had been developing since his early days as a Marxist.

Eccentric in appearance, habits and speech, Brecht eschewed middle-class comfort as well as material values; his 'uniform' of military-type leather jacket and cap, his bristling, close-cropped head, unshaven chin, and cheap foul-smelling cigars all suited the proletarian image. Brecht preferred the company of men whose aims were active and tangible, like engineers and explorers, to those whose temperament inclined them to the sedentary creativity of the arts, and he brought an understanding of professional opinions and attitudes to his portrayal of a divided society. Nevertheless, people of different persuasions, whatever their political or social outlook, found that they had to take account of his theatrical vision and poetic lyricism.

Brecht was not essentially a party politician, but an ideologist and a practical man of the theatre who sought to restore to that eminently public art a true social function; he wished to reinvest drama with the capacity to make men see clearly the way in which they live, to judge themselves, and if necessary to take vital decisions to change their mode of life. For him theatre was a living force, a force of change, and he intended that, like the Elizabethan theatre, it should be a social rallying-point; on his stage, correctives for the over-endowed and incentives for the underprivileged could be implied in the action. His didactic intentions were never concealed; indeed he wrote articles and pamphlets in demonstration of his views and appended Notes to his plays which illustrated their central purpose.

Fortunately for Brecht and for drama, he was a marvellously appreciative man, who swallowed whole and with gusto many of the simpler forms of stage and screen entertainment. He loved German music hall and cabaret of the 1920s and 1930s, and saw countless American musicals during his wartime exile. In fact for some he is best-known for his collaboration with Kurt Weill on such musical works as *The Threepenny Opera*. When he began to write a play, the colloquial and concrete were his starting-points, not high-flown rhetoric or the abstractions of theory. He also had a great appetite for information, which resulted in his collecting not so much a library as huge piles of newspaper cuttings that were a constant reminder to him of present and changing realities. The expression onstage of this changing world exercised his vast range of talent; Brecht could hold his audience by the careful selection and juxtaposition of physical detail, brute language, clear prose, song and poetic lyric. His characters possess a sheer physicality in the theatre, which perhaps comes as a shock to the reader of the plays who, if he did not see them in their proper dramatic context, might imagine them to be amalgams of slogan and propaganda. Brecht was a master craftsman with the craftsman's desire to produce a satisfying object. As others worked with wood, clay or metal, he worked at close quarters with actors and stage to realise something earthy, useful and pleasing.

Given his over-riding concern with the ordinary working man, it is not surprising to learn that Brecht had a lifelong admiration for Büchner. Inspired by the ideals of the French Revolution, Büchner had himself been an active objector and revolutionary. But fidelity to contemporary truth did not allow him to show his peasant hero as other than a passive and tormented victim. A century later Brecht could depict members of the working class as men of action, for both the long-drawn-out and painful Industrial Revolution and the Communist Revolution in Russia had instructed the masses in their powers of united action. Brecht's claim to originality is that he invented a theatre of statement, in which he exposed each and every man's need to define himself in a positive and, if need be, challenging relationship with society. Woyzeck's spiritual descendants are to be found in these Brechtian characters who move towards self-determination.

In order to implement his concept of theatre Brecht evolved on the one hand a combination of technical devices and, on the other, a mode of acting appropriate to his didactic requirement. Primarily, he wished to confront his spectators with a deliberately theatrical phenomenon which contained no pretence, no attempt at illusion. Stage-lighting was to be prominent and harsh, the machinery of effects left visible, and change of time and place indicated by placard or other obvious convention. The idea that we should 'suspend disbelief' when we watch drama was supplanted by its polar opposite: we should be continually and intensely aware that what we are watching is a theatrical event. One way of achieving this was by projecting slides on to a screen behind the actors, thus adding silent visual comment to the dialogue material or extending the considerations arising from it. Another was to reinforce or question the narrative by interspersing it with songs providing a direct commentary on the progress of the action. Everything should combine to say to the audience: 'Look! You are in the theatre. What do you think of this?'

As regards the mode of acting, Brecht rebelled against the age-old dramatic tradition, which sought to involve the audience wholly in what was happening on stage, and to cast such a spell over the spectator that he identified completely with the hero in his trials or achievement. Brecht insisted that his actors should abandon the idea of 'living a part', of entering into a character to such an extent that they assumed its personality and purpose and entirely lost their own. By means of exercises and endless repetition, Brecht taught the actor how to maintain a certain distance from his role. First, like any good modern teacher from Stanislavsky to the American exponents of the Method, he encouraged the player to absorb himself in his character in order to reach complete understanding; then, he got him to preface his lines with 'he said', turning the speech into the third person and past tense, or to exchange parts with other actors. All this put things into a new perspective, and in the place of total subjective involvement there would emerge a critically objective presentation of a role. It is true to say that the Brechtian actor must be both Hamlet and a questioning witness of Hamlet; he must accept this contradiction and not try to resolve it. Alternating involvement and judgement, he will not conceal from the audience that he has thought about the event in which he is engaged and that he is aware of its implications. 'The Chinese actor', Brecht wrote, 'watches himself act. Mimicking the unexpected appearance of a cloud, his unfolding soft and powerful, his metamorphosis rapid though imperceptible, he turns now and again to his audience as if to say: "It's like that, isn't it?"'

The television actors had to feel their way towards this duality. Equally, the director of *The Exception and the Rule* had to achieve the famous 'distancing effect' which one associates with all Brecht's work, by means of the technical devices at his disposal in the studio. He had simultaneously to make the viewer aware that he was watching an artificially contrived performance and to grip him with the truth demonstrated by the action.

The Exception and the Rule is one of a number of short plays that Brecht wrote in the early 1930s and to which he gave the name 'Lehrstücke', that is, works that instruct or teach, usually translated as 'didactic plays'. He was at that period an enthusiastic young revolutionary, out to show the error and corruption of bourgeois capitalist society. This play deals with the way in which an unjust society endorses the attitude of its 'respectable' members towards the underdog, however violent and unjustified that attitude may be: it presents the story of a desert journey on which a Merchant kills his Coolie, and of the subsequent court judgement which dismisses the Widow's claim for compensation. By implication, we are invited to condemn both the behaviour of the master towards his inferior and the processes of law which uphold the master's conduct and leave the victims of it destitute.

The Merchant bullies the overburdened Coolie (Ben Kingsley).

The adaptation to studio conditions of Brechtian theatre methods is particularly interesting. The overall technique of 'distancing' the viewer and preventing him from losing himself in the story is achieved in the first instance by the use of the bare studio floor, on which there is no pretence whatsoever of creating a realistic set. There is no mock-up of desert scene, outpost or inn, no change of scenery as such, but one or two black and white slides projected on to a free-standing screen at the back, against which the actors appear as they enter and leave. The isolated pictures make a series of simple pronouncements: 'this is a desert', 'this is an inn'. When figures pass in front of the black and white photographs the viewer automatically records the fact that they have come to the place depicted. It is an artificial convention that reminds us of the contrivance of the staged play.

Another device which Brecht embodied in his text, in order to cut across the narrative and break 'realistic' continuity, was that of interspersing the action with songs. Singing is the characters' way of explaining their motives or justifying themselves, or even of speaking for the playwright in so far as they shed objective light on events. At such moments in the television programme, the actor comes forward purposefully, advancing on the camera and on us, in order to articulate clearly – and musically – his message. The music is important. Its strong rhythms and strident tone derive from the harsh music heard in Germany's political cabaret of the 1920s and 1930s. Dee Griffiths is projected on the screen in the background in black and white film playing the piano – a nightclub honky-tonk operator, backed by a silver-shimmering slash curtain, accompanying a story of life and death. Sometimes the picture is a close-up of only the keyboard, slanting diagonally across the screen, with his hands striking out the abrasive music.

Within this convention, the conflict in the didactic drama is worked out. For most of the play it concerns the Merchant and the Coolie. The Merchant, who will go to any lengths to reach the oil in the desert before the rival party, including exploiting his Coolie and beating him on his broken arm, is played with concentrated commitment by Patrick Troughton. As the journey becomes harder, he is ever more cruel to the Coolie, and hence ever more distrustful of him, until the moment when he kills him. Ben Kingsley, who plays the Coolie, radiates the sweet, unsuspecting nature of a man who is so far from expecting to be ill-treated that he accepts everything that is done to him; but he also distances himself in Brechtian style, so that when we see him sagging with exhaustion as he drags himself across the desert under his burden, we are aware of a Brechtian irony. Malcolm Terris, as the Guide who leaves Merchant and Coolie to complete their journey on their own and tries unsuccessfully to prompt the Coolie to defiance, gives an impression of inflexible hostility as the interpreter of the dark side of capitalism represented by the Merchant. The Merchant, says the Guide, is not going to make profits from using the oil for the benefit of people, but to make money out of shutting up the wells. But, as the Coolie points out, the Guide can dare to be critical, because he is a member of a union, which the Coolie is not. Malcolm Terris's acting admirably fits the Brechtian scheme of things.

Those three mainly carry the burden of conflict in the play. The problem represented by that conflict is resolved in the final court scene by the Judge who rejects the claim of the widow after the Merchant has killed the Coolie. He is played by Denholm Elliott, who brings to the part an urbane, self-regarding pomposity which is exactly right for such a Judge. The Merchant shot the Coolie dead because he thought that the Coolie was attacking him with a stone, when in fact he was holding out a water-bottle to his tormentor. Since the Merchant had ill-treated him, rules the Judge, he was only acting reasonably in expecting the Coolie to attack him. Irony could hardly be heavier, but it is offered dead-pan, as it should be. 'The Exception' of the title is the humanity of the Coolie under oppression, and 'The Rule' is both the abuse of common decency by the Merchant as capitalist, and the absurd law which rationalises his behaviour. Brecht's last word is his advice:

> Recognise the rule which is an abuse
> And wherever you have recognised the abuse,
> Try to change it.

Merchant shoots … Coolie offering water-bottle.

Waiting for Godot by Samuel Beckett
Act II

Vladimir (Didi)	Max Wall
Estragon (Gogo)	Leo McKern
Pozzo	Graham Crowden
Lucky	Basil Clarke
A Boy	Toby Page
Designer	Colin Bowles
Director	Richard Callanan

Illustration: *Gogo (Leo McKern) lullabied by Didi (Max Wall)*.

Samuel Beckett
Waiting for Godot (1952)

Waiting for Godot is that rare thing – the origin of a contemporary myth. Godot has become part of our vocabulary. People refer to the character as easily as to Lear or Hamlet; that is to say, in complete confidence that the reference and its implication will be seized immediately.

As the play is only about twenty-five years old, compared with the three and a half centuries of Shakespearian survival, this trust in the symbol of Godot is astonishing. What is more surprising is that he is not a dramatic presence at all, but a theatrical 'absence', a character who never turns up, and cannot therefore leave upon the audience, as Lear and Hamlet do, the indelible impression of their unique humanity.

Beckett's drama leaped the successive hurdles of world success with a speed that amazed, even in an electronic age. It was a box office and theatrical 'bomb'; it received rapid intellectual recognition as a literary piece, and common emotional acceptance across continents. Works of literature – that is, works of art dependent on words – meet innumerable barriers of communication and national understanding, even when excellently translated. Ibsen's writings required time and sympathetic interpretation as they slowly spread and educated, in a dramatic sense, a gradually comprehending audience. Beckett seemed to take all obstacles at one bound, in spite of the puzzlement he aroused. *Godot* got through: to convicts in an American prison, to liberal democracies and communist societies, to progressive professionals in theatre workshops and to a vast theatre-going public. People may have felt disorientated on first acquaintance with Beckett's idle tramps, but they stayed to get to know them better. The play said something quite new in terms of drama – but age-old in ordinary human terms – and said it in a totally original way. It was all of a piece, indivisible, funny and desperately sad, and it gave to language a new name for the source of all mystery, all waiting, Godot.

Its creator, Samuel Beckett (1906–), is an Irish exile who made his home in Paris in the 1930s after a very short academic career there and some years of travel in Europe. Like James Joyce, whom he knew and admired, he led the life of an expatriate writer who concentrated in his early stories on the Ireland and Irishmen he had left behind. He fought in the French Resistance during the war, and when subsequently he turned to writing for the theatre he abandoned his native language as a deliberate act and wrote in French. *Waiting for Godot* appeared originally in French and was published as a text in 1952. It was produced early in 1953 in a little theatre on the Left Bank in Paris by an avant-garde director, Roger Blin, who found himself with a great success on his hands. Beckett translated the play himself, or rather re-thought it in English, and it came to the Arts Theatre Club in London. In the next few years it was translated into more than twenty languages, and performed in Western and Eastern Europe, the United States, South America and Japan. Other plays followed: *Endgame, Happy Days, Krapp's Last Tape*; and Beckett was awarded the Nobel Prize for Literature in 1969.

The dramatic sequence in *Waiting for Godot* is very simple. On a country road by a tree two tramps wait. They are waiting for Godot, whom they do not know and will not recognise but who has, they believe, arranged to meet them there. At the end of the day a boy arrives to say that Mr Godot cannot come that evening, but will surely come tomorrow. On the evening of the following day the same boy appears, though he denies that it was he who came the day before, and repeats the same message. The tramps go on waiting.

The play is in two Acts, which take place on two consecutive days. The television programme shows the second, and it is important to remember that when someone is waiting, that is, is in a sort of limbo, one day is very much like another. So the second half of *Waiting for Godot* mirrors the first in many respects: the tramps think up ways of passing the time, they eat, doze, dream, or invent games, according to their needs and moods. Only the fact that at the beginning of Act Two one or two green leaves are on the formerly bare tree indicates that time has gone by: this token of time passing is confirmed by the reappearance of two grotesque visitants, Pozzo and Lucky, whose arrival, as master and slave respectively, was the one 'event' of the first Act. On their return visit Lucky, now dumb, tows his erstwhile master along by the rope that used to be round his own neck. For Pozzo has gone blind and is totally dependent on the silent servant whom he used to dominate and abuse, jerking him into cowed obedience at a twitch of the lead.

At the opening of Act Two in this production, an old tramp in a bare bright place sings a grim, doggy rhyme; he wanders by a tree with one or two fluttering leaves outlined against a clear blue sky. His old brown jacket hangs on him, and in close-up his battered hat frames a world-weary face with red-rimmed eyes and tired skin. His gestures are slow and somehow without weight. The voice is gentle and musing and he looks kind. He is joined by a grumpy companion, fatter, heavier, whose bare feet plod solidly across the stage. They embrace, this ludicrous-seeming and ill-assorted pair, in the relief of reunion after a night apart. Yet they would appear to have been together not only the previous day, but for many days and years before that. Their names in the text and cast list are Vladimir and Estragon but they always refer to each other as Didi and Gogo respectively. Didi, the slighter and more adaptable of the two, is concerned for Gogo, who cries like a wilful errant child: 'Don't speak to me! Stay with me! … You let me go'. Didi is capable not only of comforting him, but also has greater internal reserves on which he can himself fall back: 'I missed you … and at the same time I was happy.' He is not completely self-sufficient for, like a lover, he pleads with the big, fat booby beside him, 'Say you are [happy], even if it is not true.' Here are a couple of lonely outcasts who need each other.

Max Wall as Didi and Leo McKern as Gogo seem to find their natural dramatic habitat in these complementary roles. They offer together a piece of miraculously sensitive playing which captures in tone, rhythm and humour the essence – the essential meaning and spirit – of Beckett's text. They are themselves men no longer young, slipping complete into the skin of old tramps, who are in fact ageless clowns, buffoons, vagrants, poets – naked human beings. The two actors with their long experience of the stage appear instinctively to know that they can entrust themselves to the flow of Beckett's lyrical prose; they let the language and the gestures it evokes take them without visible effort or straining from one moment to another. Without startling emphasis or shock tactics, they project every shade and subtlety of a dialogue which ranges from music-hall or circus cross-talk to the sad poetry of contemporary confusion and uncertainty.

Both players have the capacity to distance themselves, when required, from what they are saying and doing, which rightly reflects the characters' ability to look back on their own fooling and trivial preoccupations with sudden insight. Gogo varies from self-absorption in his own terrors, nightmares and longings for food and comfort, to wry comment on both himself and Didi. The latter at times obliterates his own feelings in concern for Gogo's needs, yet you can always see them both thinking and emoting at what goes on in their brains and bodies. That is the gift of the clown, to express inner complexities – the whizz of half-formed thought, the fleeting focus of passing emotions – in clear, external signals, connected runningly. Traditionally the clown believes himself to be deeper, nearer to the fount of life than the tragedian, and thinks that he is more serious than Hamlet and could therefore play him better than an Olivier or a Gielgud.

Didi and Gogo reveal their closeness to the tragic fount when they decide to 'try and converse calmly', seeing that they are 'incapable of keeping silent'. They talk deliberately, hoping neither to think nor to hear:

Vladimir:	We have our reasons.
Estragon:	All the dead voices.
Vladimir:	They make a noise like wings.
Estragon:	Like leaves.
Vladimir:	Like sand.
Estragon:	Like leaves.

At moments like this the dialogue becomes poetry for two voices, and the sad, elusive strain reflects their, and perhaps our, plight.

As they get through the day or evening together, Didi and Gogo divide between them, each according to his temperament, the various roles and functions people inherit or undertake in the course of a lifetime: Didi plays parent to Gogo's child, teacher to his pupil, leader and protector to his clumsy, frightened protégé. He confronts his pessimism with a tempered optimism. When Gogo fails to recall the past, Didi patiently encourages him to remember; he points out the wound on his leg where Lucky kicked him the day before, knowing that the child and brute simpleton in Gogo will be most likely to recall pain and violence. The positive thinker in Didi tries to reconstruct a past for them both, so that they can confirm their present reality by reference to what hap-

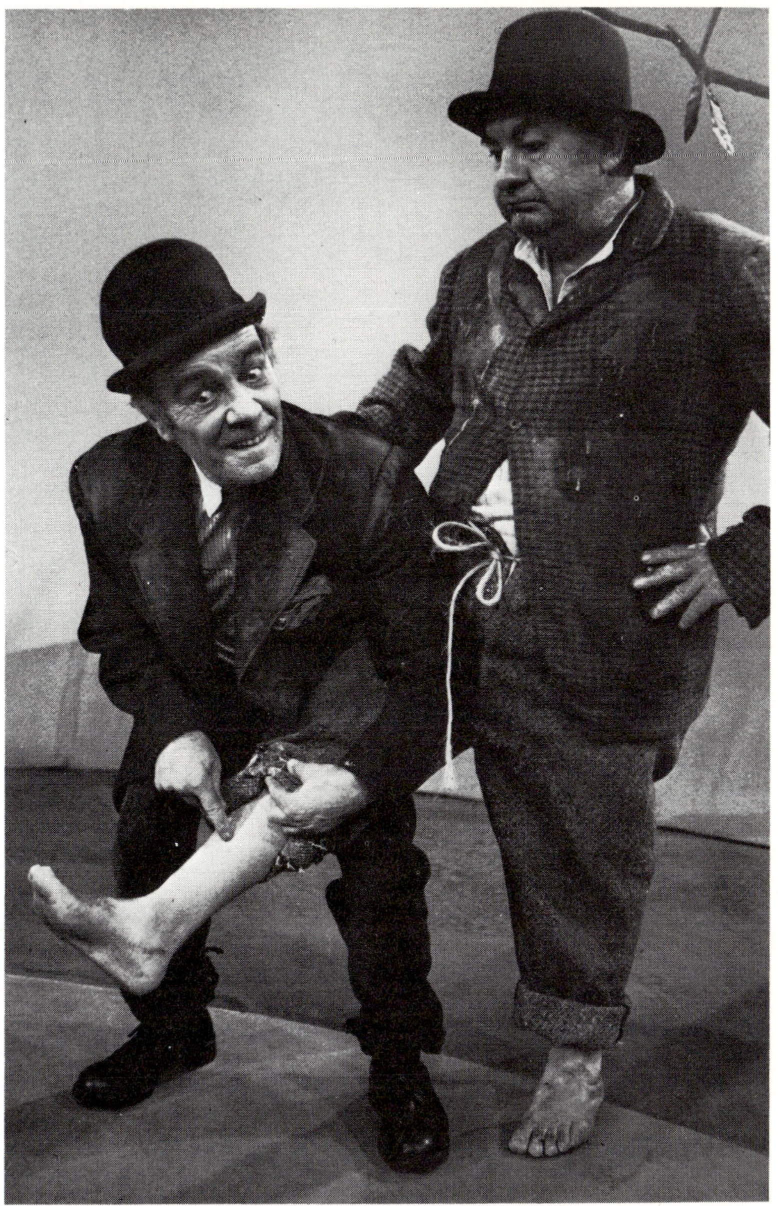

Didi reminds Gogo where Lucky kicked him.

pened before. And he does not entirely fail, for in a rare flash of understanding Gogo says: 'We always find something, eh, Didi, to give us the impression that we exist?' As friends, companions, even lovers, they enact scenes of parting and reunion, quarrel and reconciliation, encouragement and support in moments of distress. One is reminded of a scene in Strindberg's *Ghost Sonata*, although the two plays are completely different in dramatic inspiration and texture; in the hyacinth room the Student and the Daughter live through all the stages of a marriage from falling in love to death and parting. In *Waiting for Godot* there is no comparable sense of development through time, but our changing functions and attitudes to life are there separated out and isolated in a non-chronological sequence of interchanges, which have their own poetic logic.

The eruption of Pozzo and Lucky, a second couple whose reversible master-slave relationship illuminates by contrast the shared partnership of the tramps, is essential to the structure of the play and gives point and direction to its internal logic. Graham Crowden gives Pozzo a pale, bad-tempered fixity and Basil Clarke plays Lucky with a drooling, suffering dumbness. Such grotesques allow us to see Didi and Gogo's natural humanity; the two pairs are in sharp visual contrast. But in addition, they interact. Lucky's misfortune, symbolised by his lying motionless and wordless after he stumbles under Pozzo's weight in the second Act, brings out the worst in Gogo. His instinct to take revenge for a previous injury and to vent his feelings in violence on the helpless, recumbent figure is a reminder of how we act 'in society'. Gogo's brutal blows indicate only too clearly how man may react to an opportunity for naked self-assertion. Didi, on the other hand, is inclined to listen to the sentimental but pointed philosophising of Pozzo, cruel master turned blind dependant: '. . . one day he went dumb, one day I went blind . . . one day we were born, one day we shall die, the same day, the same second . . . They give birth astride of a grave, the light gleams an instant, then it's night once more.'

Much in the relationship between the couples is inexpressible, but infinitely demonstrable in terms of mime and action. There are passages of sheer physical interplay, as when Didi and Gogo struggle to get Gogo into his boots, or swap hats like children absorbed in a rhythmical game of musical hats. They may be trying on identities at the same time as they try on head-gear – in which case it is interesting that the more flexible Didi plumps for Lucky's abandoned hat and continues to wear it – but at the same time they are making contact with one another. In

Lucky (Basil Clarke) towing the blind Pozzo (Graham Crowden).

rather the same way Didi takes off his jacket and puts it round the shoulders of the slumbering Gogo, when the latter wearies of their talk. Didi is silently expressing love, even as he walks up and down flapping his arms to keep warm, and then walks Gogo patiently back and forth on the latter's brusque and terrified awakening from nightmare. Similarly the verbal games that they play – story-telling, abusing one another, analogies – express their desire to connect with one another. What waiting really requires – and we may think of the space between birth and death as a waiting – is thought, action and love-sharing. These two are beyond the pale of direct action and creative thought; but out there in the waste land on the fringe of purposeful endeavour, in comic acts and pathetic attempts to cope with their poor, punished bodies and troubled minds, they register the fundamental concerns of the human race.

The Balcony by Jean Genet
Translated by Bernard Frechtmann
A shortened version of the whole.

Madame Irma	Vivien Merchant
Chief of Police	Edward Judd
Bishop	Richard Henry
Judge	John Bryans
General	Richard Beale
Carmen	Katharine Schofield
Roger	Ronald Forfar
Penitent	Pauline Peart
Thief	Anna Bergman
Horse	Lucinda Gane
Executioner	Dave Prowse
Chantal	Christine Kimberley
Slave	Danny Schiller
Designer	David Hitchcock
Director	Nick Levinson

Illustration: *Madame Irma (Vivien Merchant) as Queen is fascinated by the success of the Chief of Police (Edward Judd).*

Jean Genet
The Balcony (1956)

The details of Jean Genet's early life read like a contemporary allegory
of a journey through hell. He was born in Paris in 1910. He was abandoned by his mother, who is thought to have been a common prostitute,
and brought up at the expense of the state by peasant foster parents.
He began to steal at the age of ten, spent much of his adolescence in
remand homes, escaped from one such *maison correctionelle* to join the
Foreign Legion when he came of age, but quickly deserted to live on
male prostitution, pilfering and petty crime. His insight into his own
motives and reasons for living in this way betrays his intelligence: 'Abandoned by my family, I found it natural to aggravate this fact by the
love of males, and that love by stealing, and stealing by crime, or complicity with crime.'

He continued to scrape an existence as a homeless outcast, going from
one country to another in order to avoid police arrest. At the time of
the German occupation he was back in France, but continually in and
out of prison for various criminal activities. It was in prison that he
started to write: first poetry in a strange, ritualistic style; then prose
poems which recounted tales of homosexual outlaws, sordid and brut-
ally explicit in subject matter but lyrical in beauty of expression. As the
title of one of these works, *Our Lady of the Flowers*, suggests, he used
the language of religious fervour and ecstasy to describe the intimacy
and pain of homosexual love affairs and violent jealousies.

When Genet came to write his first play, *Deathwatch*, he was still preoccupied with the intense little world he knew so well – the prison cell and its isolated inmates. But through the more objective form of the drama, as compared with the highly autobiographical and subjective form of his fiction, he showed that he could fight free from his haunting obsessions and externalise a view of society that was at once wider in application and more accessible to general experience.

His next play, *The Maids*, was the first to be given public performance in 1947. This dramatic essay in role-playing, which prepared the way for *The Balcony*, was given a stylised production by France's leading actor-director, Louis Jouvet, and impressed the informed and attentive theatre-lovers of the French capital. But *Deathwatch*, the earlier play, which was put on as a result of Jouvet's success with *The Maids*, provoked a public scandal. It depicted a trio of homosexual convicts who tended, like Sartre's characters in *In Camera*, to form an eternal triangle in their inescapable cell. The ideal to which his three lesser criminals aspired was represented by a man who had committed the worst possible offence, violent, premeditated murder.

Eight years later, in 1956, Genet completed *The Balcony*. Memories of the earlier scandal lingered on, and the new work was given its first performance in an English version at the Arts Theatre Club in London in April 1957. The original plan was to follow up the London production with a Paris première at the Théâtre Antoine under Peter Brook's direction. However, Genet's reputation as a dramatist was such that the directors of the theatre were warned by the Prefect of Police that if they put on *Le Balcon*, the resulting scandal would force them to close down. This was tantamount to an official ban, which was not lifted until Genet won wide critical acclaim and was awarded the 'Prix de la Critique' in 1959 for his play with an entirely coloured cast, *The Blacks*. Now his work was no longer taboo.

In *The Balcony* Genet experimented with an open type of theatre in which broad themes took precedence over intricacies of plot and character psychology. Impressed by the work of Brecht, who brought his company to Paris in 1955, he retained a continuous sequence of event and his own distinctive lyricism, but began consciously to exploit the visual, non-linguistic aspects of drama – startling, colourful spectacle, stylised movement that approached ritual or mime, sound effects and music. Like Antonin Artaud, who produced a revolutionary theory of drama in the 1930s, his concept of a 'theory of cruelty', Genet came to believe that theatre could operate on a second plane above that of the ostensible dramatic action: there, it found its 'double', to use Artaud's famous term, in metaphysics, primitive myth or fundamental cruelty. At this level the savagery and barbarism illuminated by the dramatic action were meant to drain the audience of the poisons that contaminated their being; and by forcing this process, they helped people to recognise, and drop if necessary, their masks of social and political role-playing. Genet sees human nature as infinitely corrupted and corruptible, but records it splendidly in its filth and degradation. In *The Balcony* he uses the theme of the masks we assume in public and in private in order to meditate theatrically with variations upon levels of reality.

The television programme presents a condensed version of *The Balcony*, which gives, as it happens, prominence to the opening scenes, and only one scene is not represented. At the start we see a sumptuously robed and mitred bishop engaged in grandiloquent, theological discourse. The resplendent figure, as one is abruptly made to realise, is not a bishop absolving a penitent in a cathedral, but a gas-man enacting a private fantasy in a brothel with a prostitute, for whose services he pays her employer, Madame Irma. In adjoining rooms other men live out other 'dreams': a judge passes sentence on an imploring girl-thief and watches her being whipped in punishment; and a general rides into battle on his favourite horse – a beautiful girl – and, on his death, she draws the gun-carriage bearing his body. All three have two kinds of speech and

The 'dead' General (Richard Beale) with his 'horse' (Lucinda Gane) amid military paraphernalia in the brothel.

behaviour – those appropriate to their assumed roles, and their own, as complaining, bargaining or frightened customers.

The 'Grand Balcony', to give the brothel its full title, is not only a house of ill repute; it is also a theatre. Its private rooms, hired out by the hour, resemble stage-sets in which clients find the necessary properties, scenery, costume and 'actresses' to enable them briefly to live out their aspirations and illusions. Such is the theatre itself – a place of stage events, of rehearsal and repeated action, where imagination takes precedence over insignificant actuality. As its discerning director, Madame Irma, says: 'The Grand Balcony has a world-wide reputation. It's the most artful yet the most decent house of illusions.' Genet has drawn his spectators into a brothel, only to make clear that it is an image of the theatre where all play appropriate roles. Does he go one stage further and come near to showing that this theatre is an image of the outside world itself?

The plot of the play – although it might be more accurate in the case of such a loosely-structured drama to speak of a 'story-line', as in the works of Brecht which were equally episodic – hinges on the fact that revolution rages in the city outside. Firing can be heard in the opening scenes in the bedrooms. We learn that the queen, a distant figure in a remote palace with her entourage of generals, bishops and judges, is under attack from young revolutionaries. Their leader, a plumber called Roger, has been to the Grand Balcony on a job, where one of Madame Irma's girls, Chantal, met and fell in love with him. The insurgents have turned her into the symbol of their cause, and she leads them into battle. Against them the Chief of Police pits his practical know-how and insight into mob psychology. Ruthless, pragmatic and utterly self-seeking, he realises that he will only have proof of his power over the mass mind when one man, one single representative of the subservient State, comes to the brothel asking to impersonate the Chief of Police. That day he will have 'won'; it will mark his apotheosis as a cult figure, a 'myth'.

Meanwhile the royal palace, the queen and her officials are destroyed. Madame Irma and her customers are asked by the Envoy, a survivor of the royal entourage, to play the parts of queen, general, judge and bishop in public so that the easily swayed crowd may see with their own eyes that these embodiments of authority are alive. They appear solemnly on the balcony acknowledging the crowd. The trick works, the insurrection is put down, and Chantal is killed in the flurry and confusion. Now the 'bishop', 'judge' and 'general' must act out their parts in reality. Much as they long for their fantasy worlds again, they are impelled to strive for the power and prestige implied by their titles and status. But George, the Chief of Police, is quick to remind them that they are but puppets; the real authority lies elsewhere – he thinks of himself as king- or queen-maker. He and Madame Irma operate from her house a virtual dictatorship, yet George will not feel safe until he and his function have become the centre of some client's erotic daydream. He hopes that an immense mausoleum under construction in the city will be his memorial, and the 'tomb room' in the brothel is intended as its studio replica.

George's wishes are gratified when Roger, the defeated revolutionary leader, arrives to act out the fiction that he is Chief of Police. Unknown to himself, he is watched on monitors in a control room as he declares 'I've a right to lead the character I have chosen to the very limit of his destiny – no, of mine – of merging his destiny with mine'. So saying, he pulls out a knife and castrates himself. George, his apotheosis achieved, retires to spend the rest of time in the brothel mausoleum. As gunfire announces a new rebellion, Madame Irma sends all her clients – and her audience – home, for she must divest herself of her regal attire and reassume her original role as director of the house of illusions.

The question that remains at the end of the play – which is emphasised rather than solved by Madame Irma's last words, '. . . you must now go home, where everything – you can be quite sure – will be false than here . . .' – is: where, in life, does one reach a point beyond fantasy, beyond role-playing, beyond pretence, at which one touches at last on reality? At moments in the play the spectator doubts whether the world outside the Grand Balcony really exists. Admittedly gunfire is heard; clients, prostitutes and household staff exchange information about the progress of the revolution – 'This afternoon, just before you arrived, the rebels took three key positions'; Chantal is shot and Roger, abandoning in defeat his ideological revolutionary stance, turns to glorification of a police regime. And yet the revolution and its trail of fire and destruction are described often in strangely symbolic, even mystic language. 'There's blood everywhere,' says Irma to the 'bishop' in the first studio scene, and he repeats, 'You say the city's splashed with blood'. 'Everything went up in flames,' they explain to the 'judge'; and yet when the Envoy arrives to recruit his new symbols of power, he will give no definite news about the collapse of the monarchy. 'From something or other about the explosion,' he remarks, 'from its power, in which was mingled a clinking of jewels and broken mirrors, I rather think it was the royal palace.' He refers to the supposedly dead queen first as 'embroidering', later as being 'in a chest. She is sleepy. Wrapped in the folds of royalty she is snoring.' And when Irma, who is to take on the mantle of the sovereign, says: 'So, I'll be real? My robe will be real! My lace, my jewels will be real! The rest of the world ...', one notes immediately that she does not finish the sentence and that she questions her own reality in the new role; but the authentic trappings give her pleasure and confidence. We remember the Envoy's phrase about 'the clinking of jewels' at the time of the explosion, and fear that Irma's ornaments will prove equally impermanent. As for her incomplete sentence, 'the rest of the world ...', here we are at the heart of the existential problem and Genet leaves it unanswered.

The method Genet adopts is to scatter the play with visual clues to his way of viewing 'the world'. In each room in the brothel a large mirror with a carved, gilt frame reflects an unmade bed. The audience sees a reflection of the actors, playing the parts of clients and whores, who are pretending to be solemn public figures and their victims or servitors, in imitation of the 'real' representatives of officialdom in the world outside, a reflection of a reflection of a reflection. And the explosion which the Envoy hears contains the sound of 'broken mirrors'. But when the inmates of the dream, that mirror-world of the brothel, are drawn outside to play their roles in earnest, they do not escape from reflection to authentic being. The broken mirrors would appear to be instantly replaced, because reality is as dreamlike as the dream. George, the Chief of Police, a hardened activist whose ambition has allowed nothing to stand in its way, knows that external action is not enough to guarantee a true, as opposed to a reflected, image: 'I shall not be the hundred-thousandth-reflection-within-a-reflection in a mirror, but the one and Only, into whom a hundred thousand went to merge.' We are all images of images, whatever our function in life. To become 'true' is to become an archetype, 'the one and Only', an ideal to which the mass of humanity cannot even aspire. Most often we are like the gas-man, who plays at being a bishop: if we got the chance to play at being a real bishop, then like the gas-man we should probably prefer to revert to make-believe, for the 'reality' contains no more truth, power and authority than the dream.

This view of life is deeply anarchistic. It does not seek to destroy one social or political structure in order to replace it with another. Genet condemns equally the quasi-fascist suppression meted out by the established order, and the communistic zeal of revolutionary change. As Richard Coe has said: 'If the Right was offended by the opening scenes of *Le Balcon*, the Left was equally insulted by the sight of a revolutionary hero castrating himself in the presence of the Chief of Police, thereby acknowledging with a gesture of irremediable defeatism the failure of the revolution and the impotence of its ideals.' In fact, when the play was revived later in the 1960s, left-wing French students demonstrated violently against the anti-revolutionary attitude of the author. Genet puts his faith in no socio-political system. Unlike Brecht, he does not see the proletarian hero as 'right' and the Establishment as 'wrong'. Cunningly he places the virtues of energy, organisational ability and personal appeal on the side of the 'baddies', the repressive reactionaries, and then develops his story of repeated destruction to show that neither side can win. It is wrong to regard the play as primarily political allegory.

In the television production the early scenes are a feast of spectacle, exotic colour and verbal richness, in which each room has the luxurious fake appurtenances for its special activity. The 'bishop', wearing encrusted robes and a gold mitre, and the 'penitent', in a black veil beside the burning candles, operate in an ecclesiastical setting of purple and gold. The 'judge' in his scarlet robes crawls, pleads and sentences his victim against a background of red and gold; her hands clutch the red bars to which she is bound as the Executioner whips her to obtain her confession, and his half-naked body gleams in the dim light of the courtroom. The setting of the battlefield, where the 'general' conducts his triumphant last campaign, is green, gold and black. The khaki uniform, in which he is dressed by his beautiful companion, merges with this colour scheme as it would on the field of battle, and the girl in her flashy, black high-heeled boots and black shiny corset, with dark flowing hair and red tail, is a symbol both of his war horse and of the erotic.

Madame Irma's apartment is rich in real silks, deep, glowing colours and extravagant, feminine luxury. An exquisite black shawl with huge red flowers is draped across the sofa. She herself dresses flamboyantly to offset her hennaed hair, and is attracted by both the charms of her young 'protégées' and the masculine aggressiveness of the Chief of Police. Ambivalent, scheming, a good business woman and vulnerable lover, Irma is admirably portrayed by Vivien Merchant. She combines and subtly reconciles the characteristics of keeper of a bawdy-house, queen and worldly-wise mistress, all the while providing the inspiration behind the 'house of illusions'. The mannered playing of the Envoy (Gerald Cross) and the carefully judged alternation between radical brutality and personal fanaticism of the Chief of Police (Edward Judd) help conjure up the necessary atmosphere of ambiguity and uncertainty.

Sizwe Bansi is Dead devised by Athol Fugard, John Kani and Winston
Ntshona
All but the opening monologue.

Buntu/Styles	John Kani
Sizwe Bansi	Winston Ntshona
Designer	Michael Edwards
Producer	Graeme McDonald
Director	John Davies

Illustration: *John Kani as Buntu (left) and Winston Ntshona.*

Athol Fugard
Sizwe Bansi is Dead (1972)

This last play is like no other in the series. It is not a classic or a modern masterpiece, already fixed in dramatic history by years of performance and review and still more years of scholarly criticism. As we have it, it is not even a text in the strict sense, because the two actors freely improvise every time they perform it, and the words they speak bear only a general resemblance to those of the printed text, although the order of events is always the same. Since the play originated in workshop improvisations, and the two actors, John Kani and Winston Ntshona, are joint authors of the play with Athol Fugard, that is right. Then, there is no other play in this series which deals with one of today's burning issues, as this one deals with *apartheid*. Not that we need a play to tell us that *apartheid* is evil: a pamphlet or a speech could do that better. But to prove it on our pulses as well as in our minds, we need the help of art, and above all of dramatic art, the public one to which censors and authoritarian régimes of all colours are sensitive. Only through art – and of course documentary, which is at its best an art form – can we discover imaginatively and emotionally the human predicament lived through under regimes and their laws. *Sizwe Bansi is Dead* is not 'about' the pass laws of apartheid, but the relationship of two men brought together by the pressures of *apartheid*.

Athol Fugard has recorded how he came to play his part in *devising* (rather than writing) the play while working with Serpent Players, an African drama group in Port Elizabeth. For four years the group had been performing well-known plays, and they had gradually realised that they wanted to relate more closely to their audience than the performance of European classics allowed. So they began to improvise on subjects of interest to their audience. Since theatre in South Africa is largely segregated, and the actors, like those who watched, were black, these subjects were necessarily of specifically black concern.

Improvisation depends entirely on the actor. Imaginative and active projection of the theme is all-important, and the particular words said or things done on stage are important only for their relation to the theme as projected in one performance; at the next performance, the same theme might be developed in a slightly different way, so that different words, different actions and a different tempo might work better. Fugard's theatre is thus actor-centred, not text-centred, though he as 'author' stands in part behind the ideas, and as 'director' stands in part behind the presentation, participating as adviser. He was stimulated in this approach to his work by the ideas of the Polish director Grotowski, who trained his actors to be creative. To Grotowski, creativity in an actor means not just responding to a text with imaginative interpretation, but working on pre-textual base material – event, mood, motive – to make a new dramatic artefact. It follows, given the circumstances in which Athol Fugard, John Kani and Winston Ntshona worked, that the 'base material' with which they began had to come out of their own experience. In a way, that would seem to ensure that only a narrow range of subjects could be chosen for making plays; but since their racial experience is largely unrepresented in drama, and since almost any human experience, if profoundly and imaginatively treated, can have universal impact, it is wrong to think of a play emerging from a repressed group of people under *apartheid* as necessarily having limited relevance. It would be more justifiable to brand English drawing-room comedy as a genre of limited possibilities, because it has been in existence for so long that it must have used up all its potential.

The key experience behind *Sizwe Bansi is Dead*, though by no means the only important one, is the work Fugard had done twenty years before in a Native★ Commissioner's Court on Pass Law cases. For a white man of liberal sympathies, it must have been unbearable to be a cog in a machine which, according to his account, sent one man to gaol every two minutes of the working day for passbook irregularities. The event celebrated and dwelt on with increasingly joyous certainty throughout

★ The word 'Native' is deeply offensive to blacks because it is not used of whites. Even the South African government has now dropped it.

the play, the central subject, is the success of Sizwe Bansi in taking over the identity of a dead man, Robert Zwelinzima, together with Zwelinzima's passbook entitlement to work in Port Elizabeth, from which Bansi has just been banished by the withdrawal of his work permit.

Another important experience used in the play is John Kani's period of work on a Ford assembly line. It is capitalised in the long speech by the photographer Styles which begins the play. He describes, with a lot of vigorous mimic action, how he became debased by the factory system and especially by the bosses with their covert tyranny and false promises; how at times he salved his self-respect by making fools of them, and how at last he managed to escape that automatic-monkey, white-dominated life, and to set up as a photographer. Styles then with great humour makes his serious point that the photographer by catching happy moments, and especially smiles, for eternity, consoles people for their wretched lives: 'There is nothing we can leave behind when we die, except the memory of ourselves.' That opening narration, which is not included in the television programme, sets the tone and the action frame for the rest of the play, all of which we see.

The third experience which went into the making of the play was an art experience rather than a life one – if such a distinction may be made. Athol Fugard says that the starting-point of *Sizwe Bansi is Dead* was his fascination with a studio photograph he 'had once seen of a man with a cigarette in one hand and a pipe in the other'. In the play Sizwe Bansi, who already calls himself Robert Zwelinzima, comes to Styles's studio to have a photograph taken so that he may send it to his wife, in happy celebration of his new identity. And this is the photograph that is taken. The blissful smile, the cigarette in one hand and the pipe in the other, symbolise Bansi's delight at outwitting the Pass Laws. Styles persuades 'Robert' to have another photograph taken, and when the flashlight goes off, there is a blackout except for one light on 'Robert'.

We are in a new dimension, for 'Robert', who is illiterate, is dictating his happy letter to his wife, and starts to explain how a man called Buntu helped him to get his new identity. The dimension changes again as the letter-dictating pauses: Styles has become Buntu, and the rest of the play, apart from 'Robert's' resumption of his pose at the very end, presents the moving but often very funny interaction of the two. Buntu first explains to Sizwe Bansi, as he is at this point, the consequences of losing his work permit. Then they go to a shebeen and, as they leave it half drunk, Buntu relieves himself on what he thinks is a pile of rubbish. But it is a dead man. With half an intention of taking his body to his home,

Robert Zwelinzima (Winston Ntshona) posing for his photograph.

they take his passbook. Buntu, who can read, notices that the dead man has a work permit for Port Elizabeth. They abandon the corpse, with especial compunction on Sizwe's side ('Would you leave me lying there, wet with your piss?'), but take the passbook. In the next scene, Buntu pastes Sizwe's passbook photograph into Robert's passbook, and Robert's into Sizwe's. 'Robert' is sad at losing his name, but allows Buntu to rehearse him in his new role, with his new N.I. (Native Identity) number. The transformation is complete, and the play may end. The letter to 'Robert's' wife is finished off, and with a click we are back to the pose for the camera and Styles's musical cajoling: 'Now smile, Robert … Smile … Smile …'

Sizwe Bansi is Dead is what actors call a 'two-hander', a play for two actors only. Like *Waiting for Godot*, which is almost a two-hander, it is short on plot but long on atmosphere and relationship. There is something quite special about all two-handers in performance; the unfolding of an acting relationship which has a life of its own quite apart from the dramatic relationship of the two characters the actors are playing. And the two relationships reinforce each other. The acting relationship seems like a love relationship because of the close and continuous interaction of the two, even if the play characters are at loggerheads.

Here, the acting relationship works in a novel way. Winston Ntshona is the fixed Man, Sizwe Bansi, full of fine human feelings and suffering in his predicament (because his passbook trick will serve him only until the police examine him, at which point it will be discovered that his finger-prints do not tally with those of the nominal holder of the passbook). John Kani is the photographer, who becomes Buntu; and Buntu, as he coaches Sizwe, becomes successively a Native Commissioner telling Sizwe to report to King William's Town, a white lady interviewing him for a garden boy's job, a lay preacher burying an old black man, a white man giving out pay packets at the Feltex factory, a salesman, a priest enrolling Sizwe in a burial society, and a policeman checking his passbook. The partnership is thus between a centre, a planet man whose joys and miseries are the prime emotional focus in the play, and a periphery, a succession of dazzling satellite men all with the same face. This explains why, although there seems to be every reason for a third actor to play Buntu, the play is best contained within the single relationship. That 'same face' of John Kani, with its many faces, and its two dominant characters, Styles the dynamic intuitive whizz-kid photographer and Buntu the experienced politico, provides the frame for the focus on Sizwe Bansi.

Although the single event of the play is a joyous one, the prevailing mood is of furious defiance of the entire system under which black people live in South Africa, and of determination to survive. It is a fruitful defiance, partly because of the verbal and physical energy of the two men, which is nobly productive, and partly because of their humanity, which counterpoises every aspect of the oppression to which they are subject. The comprehensiveness of this oppression astonishes, and it is from Styles–Buntu, as adviser, teacher, guardian angel and in some sense torturer of Sizwe–Robert, that we learn most of the detail. He describes the tentacular reach of the passbook system: how a man must have his passbook in perfect order for every occasion – getting a job, receiving a pay packet, establishing residence, joining a burial society, and especially being stopped by a policeman. Everything depends on a person's number: 'Burn that into your head, friend ... It's more important than your name.' And if the passbook is not in order, then there is no bread for the stomach or blanket for winter.

All this and much more is dramatically used as argument by Buntu to make Sizwe accept the loss of his identity and become 'Robert'. If Buntu tortures Sizwe, it is only to force him to see where his best interest lies. The last few moments are memorable for the deep pain Sizwe Bansi feels at giving up his name: won't 'Sizwe Bansi is dead' mean not just a passbook exchange, but the extinction of an actual person?

What about my wife? ... Her loving husband, Sizwe Bansi, is dead! ... and my children! ... They're registered at school under Bansi.

But when he asks, 'How do I live as another man's ghost?' Buntu has the just, metaphysical, answer: the owner of a Native Identity number who can be called 'Boy' by a white child has no adult existence, no dignity, anyway:

Isn't that a ghost? Stop fooling yourself ... be a real ghost ... Spook them into hell, man!

Sizwe Bansi's responses are always less intellectual than those of Styles–Buntu. It is not the implication of a particular piece of repression that concerns him so much as his gut reaction against it. For example, when Buntu suggests that he should accept the loss of his work-permit and go down the mines, where 'they don't worry about Influx Control', Sizwe replies:

I don't want to work on the mines. There is no money there. And it's dangerous, under the ground. Many black men get killed when the rocks fall.

Last of all, when the two men are considering how long their passbook exchange trick will keep Sizwe Bansi safely working in Port Elizabeth, Buntu starts talking about staying 'out of trouble'. The word 'trouble' prompts Sizwe to the deepest, most condensed statement of the whole play:

A black man stay out of trouble? Impossible, Buntu. Our skin is trouble.

The drama deals with an oppression which can be removed, and no doubt will be, although in the very month that this book is written, John Kani and Winston Ntshona have been detained in the Transkei (an oasis of 'separate development', like the 'Ciskei' of the play, in which a pale imitation of independence may be had by blacks) for performing *Sizwe Bansi is Dead*. But the problem will turn up again and again, just as 'the stinking ghost of Robert Zwelinzima' will always be with Sizwe Bansi, and the play will speak about it, whatever form it takes. We are white, or black. We are Catholic, or Protestant. We have, or we have not. We are party members, or we are not. Differences, and people's primitive sense of difference, remain to confuse our sense of humanity and to reinforce the insidious suggestion that, because other people are different from us in some superficial way, they may not be entirely human. As the writer of the *Book of Job* wrote more than two thousand years ago: 'Man is born unto trouble, as the sparks fly upward.'